Strategic Life Plan

Becoming All God Intended You to Be and Helping Others Do the Same as a Christian Life Coach

Stan DeKoven Ph. D.

Strategic Life Plan

Becoming All God Intended You to Be and Helping Others Do the Same as a Christian Life Coach

By: Stan DeKoven Ph. D.

Copyright © 2016 Stan DeKoven

ISBN 978-1-61529-069-7

Vision Publishing
P.O. Box 1680
Ramona, CA 92065
1 800 – 9 –VISION
www.booksbyvision.org

All rights reserved. No part of this book may be reproduced in any manner whatsoever without the written permission of the author except brief quotations embodied in critical articles of review.

All scriptures are taken from the New American Standard and used by permission unless otherwise noted.

Endorsements

Dr Stan DeKoven masterfully combines academic research with contemporary tools all based on the life and teachings of Jesus to build a coaching model in his book Strategic Life Plan. Stan's way of coaching focuses on positive, healthy change in both leader and follower. If you are interested in helping others achieve life goals and fulfill their callings then you will want to have this book as a resource.

Dr Tim Hamon
President, Christian International Ministries

Dr DeKoven says, "The more People Smart you are, the higher your Emotional Quotient, and therefore the greater your success can be, in relationships." (pg 42) Strategic Life Plan - Becoming All God Intended You to Be and Helping Others Do the Same as a Christian Life Coach, gives you tools to be, "People Smart"!

A Life Coach is focused to help his or her client attain goals etc., Strategic Life Plan introduces the health factor of the client which is important for them to maintain those goals and continue to their God given potential. While this is considered an introductory work, I found it to be thorough and practical. I feel better equipped on this journey to help others as my self–understanding and "people read" skills have been recalibrated and enhanced. If you work with people at any level this book will help you to be more effective!

Mark McElwee
Pastor / Senior Leader
Heart of God Church, San Diego CA

My excellent friend, Dr. Stan, has "done the difficult"—he has breathed new life into a worn-out word, Strategic. Everyone wants a good life. Few strategize for it. Dr. Stan DeKoven has provided a fresh blueprint that *anyone* can start *now*—regardless of your age. Read, consider, digest, and employ Strategic Life Plan. Yes, you can. Why not now?

Bob Nolan, Bible Briefings / Thought Provokers

Table of Contents

Endorsements 3
Table of Contents 5
Introduction 7
Chapter 1: Coaching Defined 11
Chapter 2: The Balanced Life Philosophy: What is a Balanced Life? 27
Chapter 3: Healthy Functional Family System 41
Chapter 4: Dysfunctional Family System 49
Chapter 5: The Head: Understanding Style…and the Art of Communication 59
Chapter 6: DISC Graphs and "D's" 77
Chapter 7: All About I 85
Chapter 8: All About S 93
Chapter 9: All About C 99
Chapter 10: Read On 105
Chapter 12: Selling in Style with DISC 115
Chapter 13: The Process of Mentor/Coaching 131
Chapter 14: Getting Down to It: How Can Coaching Help? 153
Conclusion: Heart, Head and Hands 167
Appendix: Forms for Starting Your Work 169
About the Author 181

6

Introduction

I was always a better coach than player...and I was a pretty good player, in baseball that is. My skills and drive took me through my undergraduate studies at San Diego State University, but my higher call moved me to study psychology and theology at the graduate level, to pursue a life of ministry in counseling and teaching.

I always enjoyed preaching and teaching better than psychotherapy, and loved working with folks that had potential to do something significant with their life. Now, don't misunderstand me, all people have worth, but not all have equal potential. Thus, over time, my counseling, preaching, teaching and writing began to move more towards enhancing life, reaching potential, overcoming obstacles and strategic planning for the future...life coaching became my passion.

What is Life Coaching?

Life coaching is a rapidly growing field of practice and knowledge designed to assist people develop both personally and professionally. The life coach guides clients, rather than patients, toward meeting their goals and dreams. The emphasis is on "producing action and uncovering learning that can lead to more fulfillment, more balance, and a more effective process for living". Life coaching is in many ways an extension of executive coaching, with the specific goal of helping an executive achieve higher levels of success in business and life. Life coaching is in its infancy compared to professions involving psychology, social work, sociology, and business. The life coach does not have to have a degree or a certification, but it is certainly desirable. [1] A recent coaching

---

[1] This book is our (Vision International University) introduction to Christian Life Coaching, a course that can be taken towards a degree in Christian Counseling with emphasis in Life Coaching. For more information, see http://www.vision.edu/web/viu/degrees/ma_counseling

study identified "untrained individuals who call themselves coaches were viewed as the main future obstacle for coaching (Beebe & Lachmann, 2002).

Adult education is a broad term including formal college education; job related training, community education, or self-improvement. Adult education emerged from the training and development field expanding outside of organizational development to community and higher education venues. Coach training programs are adult education programs as they are targeted towards adult learners, facilitated by adult educators, and promote professional and personal development. Similar to a life coach an adult educator facilitates meaningful adult learning honoring the experiences of the adult learner. A primary purpose of adult education is to recognize adult learners as resourceful in understanding their experiences and reflecting upon them for problem-solving (Blanchard & Shula, 1995).

Life coaching and adult education share properties related to adult learning. Both were influenced by psychology and philosophy. Both focus on adult learners with the goal of transforming and enriching lives. Both recognize adult learners are self-directed and possess the characteristics of knowing what they want to achieve, as well as learn, through active participation. Life coaching is referred to as a process to enhance and change lives enabling learning and development to occur. The emphasis of life coaching is on the present and future, focused on goals and behavior (Casserley & Megginson, 2009).

I would add to this definition, which is certainly well presented, that life coaching is a form of discipleship (more on this in chapter 1). Through strategic questions and loving confrontation (presented in the appendices are samples), a coach (a mentor or discipler) assists the client in facing the truth about their lives, and adjust, both short term and long; to help them achieve, agreed upon, reachable goals. These goals include the values of the client and the gifts and calling of their life. Accomplishing these goals requires a clear philosophy and certain skills, some of which are innate, but most can be learned. The coach will focus on the philosophy, which has often been referred to as the "Balanced Life Philosophy" modified by the 5 C's of our overall coaching model.

Having a clear understanding of oneself, as well as an understanding of the other person's purpose, goals, dreams, passions, etc., is the initial element of coaching. As in other professional fields of endeavor such as medicine or psychotherapy, a good diagnosis is paramount, leading to proper treatment. Though the medical model is not an appropriate one for life coaching (it is more about wellness than sickness) a good understanding of one's own strengths and weaknesses, biases and fears, etc. as well as those of the client's is essential. What will be presented here is a model for gathering information on the client that will lay the foundation of a life plan. The primary focus will be on the dynamic DISC profile and its usage as a primary tool for coaching, presented in a later part of this book.

Because vision and goal setting are so important, as they lead to the actual implementation of the plan, separate chapters have been dedicated to these vital subjects. This should lead a reasonable person in the direction of achieving their life goals.

The final section will focus on coaching and the coach. They are designed to assist the life coach in fulfilling his own goals and dreams which, I trust, is to see many men and women step fully into their divine destiny.

"Good coaching is good teaching and nothing else."

Pat Conroy,
My Losing Season: A Memoir

Chapter 1:
Coaching Defined

Coaching is a relationship between the student and the coach. It is the essential dialogue between the student and the coach within a constructive, results-oriented framework previously agreed upon by both. The coach asks questions during the critical stages in which the student and coach collaborate for meeting the student's objectives. The agenda itself comes from the student. The student is then directed in a support-conducive environment to look at the various angles and strategies. The coach is a resource partner whose definitive goal for success is to support and assist students to reach their full potential. The coach is the student's resource to encourage the fulfillment of the potential success, in the perspective defined by the student, and in the development of an overall balance.

On a practical level, coaching is concerned with setting and achieving goals. Coaching can be a long-term or a short-term relationship between the coach and the student depending on the depth and extent of the goals. Its scope is broader than counseling in that, the coach and student are corroborating prospective plans for change and/or improvement in several specific areas of the student's life. For instance, the counselor may ask questions about a client's past, to assess their present circumstances and to explain why the client reacts a certain way. A coach may ask questions concerning present relationships and explain how to change the way they react.

Coaching, here, is not the same as sports coaching, but the two are certainly related. When a tennis player is performing on the court, the coach sits in the stands and observes every aspect of the player's game. They provide constructive guidance on how the players could improve their specific plays and help identify what happened in a game that led to losing the entire set. They can then assist in determining what to do to correct it. All coaching is similar in that the student has skills, abilities, and knowledge, which the coach needs to help develop. They provide insight and direction to reach greater potential. In short, instead of talking about sports skills, we are concerned with life skills, relationship skills, and work skills.

Traditional Role of Life Coach

Life Coaching is an interactive method to assist an individual or group in the development and achievement, to redirect them where they want to be in their personal and professional lives. Coaching is a process that helps to define who you are, what your values are and helps you move from the current position to one where a person wants to end up in life. It therefore focuses on the choices and encourages reflection, motivation and action. A life coach does not tell clients how to live their lives, but stimulates the use of efficient techniques of questioning, to make them look outside the usual solution so they will find their own optimal solution. The active support of a life coach helps clients grow faster and more efficiently than if they worked by themselves, encouraging the questioning of old patterns of behavior, while allowing the emergence of new ways of thinking and acting. A life coach often acts as a mirror in front of a client by returning a new and different perspective. The role of a life coach is to provide individuals with a way to empower themselves by controlling the progress of their action plans.

Together they evolve and find the method that best suits the client's needs. For this, the life coach uses different tools, such as investigation, reflection, requests and discussion. Coaching can help clients identify their personal goals and professional relationships, and develop strategies, relationships and action plans to achieve these goals (Phillips, 2003).

Different Aspects of Life Coaching

Higher education recognizes life coaching as an emerging discipline offering master's degrees and classes in life, business, and executive coaching. Many American universities have introduced coaching programs, including Harvard, Yale, Duke, the University of California at Berkeley, and others. Some colleges offer coaching to freshman students to help with the transition from high school to college. [2]

Although most empirical research on the significance and effectiveness is based upon studies related to Executive coaching, there are more and more studies being conducted demonstrating the positive results which can be obtained from Life Coaching.

As previously stated, the coaching industry is growing tremendously, and there are emerging studies from graduate students' research in the past three years focusing on life coaching.

A review of the literature identified several studies conducted with the executive coaching profession. Executive coaching is defined as working with someone one-on-one at an executive level within an organization. It is a challenge to compare or correlate the findings of these studies with the findings of studies on life coaching. The executive coaching studies are predominantly focused on organizational benefits such as increasing sales and managing teams, rather than on the coaches or clientele. Other studies on life coaching focused on the coaching process and what coaching approach works best. These studies supported the value of coaching. As indicated in an executive coaching research, the whole coaching journey is undertaken for the benefit of the clients, so it is certainly worthwhile to understand their perspectives as deeply as possible. As offered by another researcher on the value of life coaching, since life coaching is considered of value, this study added value in understanding the experience of critical self-reflection by life coaches (Ellis & Bochner, 1996).

---

[2] An excellent program that provides this service is "Career Direct', available through the Vision Resourcing Group, http://www.visionresourcinggroup.com/

Core Competencies of Coaching

The International Coaches Federation (ICF) developed a list of core competencies for the coaching profession and to assist in credentialing individuals through its organization. These competencies apply to any type of coaching practice whether wellness, life, business, or executive coaching. They are not ranked in any order, and they guide the individual seeking coach training to identify professional training programs, which will meet these competencies. The core competencies include:

- Meeting ethical guidelines and professional standards
- Establishing the coaching agreement
- Establishing trust and intimacy with the client
- Coaching presence
- Active listening
- Powerful questioning
- Direct communication

What is of interest is that the practice of critical self-reflection, self-evaluation, or reflection on the coach's part is not listed. In the descriptors of each core competency, no mention is made of the coach participating in self-evaluation or introspective work. These competencies are targeted towards the client, albeit credentialing depends upon whether the coach adheres to these principles in practice. Well established coach training programs will focus on these core competencies.

The Basic Forms of Coaching

There are several forms of coaching which should be mentioned. They provide valuable benefits in addition to individual and group coaching. They are: Peer coaching; Mirror coaching; Collaborative coaching; and Expert coaching.[3]

Peer Coaching is a form of coaching that provides support, feedback, and assistance from peers of the same profession. While peer coaching has been identified with academics only, it is advantageous to all professions, as peer-coaches focus on positive reactions and solutions to any possible problems. This is opposed to peer-evaluations which tend to foster feelings of intimidation. Peer coaching provides a forum in which peers can experiment with and discuss their profession with an interested partner.

Professionals who utilize peer coaching for this purpose may meet with their partners to discuss effective business strategies, review one another's current projects or other agendas that are specific to their profession. In a sense, such partners serve each other as peer consultants in a reciprocal relationship.

Peer coaching is "a confidential process through which two or more professional colleagues work together to reflect on current practices; to expand, refine, and build new skills; share ideas; teach one another; conduct classroom research; or solve problems in the workplace" (Slater and Simmons, 2001).

In summary, Peer coaching is, confidential, non-evaluative, flexible, and voluntary, based on trust and is focused on observable behaviors. Further, peer coaching goals include the development skills in a non-threatening, non-evaluative atmosphere, and to learn new ideas and approaches from colleagues. The overall objectives of peer coaching include gaining feedback from colleagues on self-identified issues, assisting colleagues in enhancing their experiences through observation and discussion and learning new skills, methods, and strategies.

---

[3] My thanks to *Tony Stoltzfus* for his permission to adapt materials from his training for this work.

In Mirror coaching, the coach records only information which the student being observed has asked the coach to collect. After the observation, the coach turns the data over to the student to analyze. This is the end of the coach's involvement. In Mirror Coaching, the student requests information while the coach collects data requested, then the coach provides data to the student for the student to reflect and act upon.

In Collaborative coaching, the coach still collects only the data specified by the student; but the data is analyzed later by the coach and the student together, in a post observation conference. The coach guides the student in self-reflection by asking questions which help the student analyze whether the lesson objectives were attained and, if not, why not.

Social science research suggests that we learn more effectively through a collaborative relationship rather than through just the coach's expert recommendations. The more the change process is self-defined, self-monitored, self-evaluated, and self-reinforced by those making the changes, the greater the likelihood of enduring effects.

To summarize, in Collaborative coaching, the student requests information, the coach collects the data requested and the coach guides the student in self-reflection (active listening).

Finally, in Expert coaching, the expert may be a mentor who works exclusively with a student. The expert is not restricted to collecting only the data specified by the student being observed. During the post-conference, the mentor guides and directs the discussion. In Expert coaching, the mentor observes the student at work, then the mentor collects the data requested and makes observation notes on the student, followed by the mentor providing the data from the observation and discusses it with the student, who will hopefully gain insight that leads to positive action.

What is a Coach?

Again, a coach is one whose job involves "systematically developing the ability and skills of an employee (or mentee) by utilizing tasks at work in a planned progression and including by the coach." (Rae, 1994)

What Do Coaches Do?

Coaches do several things, but primarily they help to identify the learning opportunities for an individual they are coaching, and help the client to set clear learning objectives while demonstrating skill, explaining why, how, and when, the skill is used. He or she is an observer of the learner, who is willing to listen, recognize and address anxieties, while using questions to establish and maintain a learner's confidence, provide opportunities for reflection, while acting as a role model and challenging the student in day-to-day considerations. These considerations include encouraging learners to extend themselves, explain the reasons for using different methods, encourage learners to practice rather than watch and thus avoid the temptation to step in and do it for the learner.

In the process of coaching the coach will assist the coachee by breaking tasks down into achievable segments which will assist the coachee in learning by thinking, noticing and reflecting, and encourage the learners to self-assess. It is important to develop the skill to know when to encourage and when to step back, as the coach is a role model for observing different skills and attitudes, and is the key encourager to the learner and rewarder of success.

The Definition of Coaching in Leadership

Coaching is the process of inspiring, encouraging, motivating, and instructing a person to unlock his or her greatest potential, to achieve their ultimate goal. The coach becomes the person's personal resource and advocate. This helps the person to grow professionally and personally.

Coaching develops the students' confidence as well as competence, and encourages them to discover their talents, gifts, and values, in the process. Coaching is a leadership development process with a high-performance leader matched with a high potential learner. It is a task oriented process of one-on-one help to lead the **learner** to develop their gifts and talents in the ministry of the church or in the structure of the organization. To build confidence and competence, a coach must:

- Actively listen
- Be honest about concerns and the lack of certain abilities
- Provide the resources necessary to effectively train the student
- Involve the student in setting goals and objectives
- Believe in, reward, and praise success

To discover talents, gifts, and values, a Coach must:

- Stimulate the student's thinking by asking questions; not by stating solutions
- Provoke the student's own ideas
- Provide scenarios that put the student in difficult situations
- Ask how the student plans to move things forward
- Expose the consequences of the student's actions
- Always provide an opportunity for the student to ask questions
- Provide the student with time to think and grow
- Never underestimate a student
- Provide feedback in the form of corrective action for the student to follow
- Trust comes with time. Do not rush the relationship

Of course, all of these goals are to be accomplished over time, within relationship, and happen "as you go"...these are general goals and cannot be forced or manipulated, and are not to be used as a checklist of success.

Types of Coaching

Most directorate and managerial coaching deals with one of the following three categories: performance coaching, skills coaching and personal coaching.

Performance coaching: Performance coaching is an individual process that improves performance through a planned program of preparation and delivery. Depending on the requirements, these include input in the areas of skill development, psychology, theoretical knowledge, interpersonal skills, ethics, lifestyle management, time management, and strategy. Although coaches may not be personally responsible for providing all the expertise in each area, their overall coaching role and responsibility is to plan and co-ordinate the various contributions of each participant into an effective individualized strategy for enhancing personal performance in relation to their job.

Skills coaching: A skill is a developed or a learned ability. One-to-one skill coaching is an approach to the personal development of the core skills a participant needs to perform his or her role. A coach must be masterful in the art of budgeting to coach in the strategy of business planning. Skills coaches must be highly experienced in performing any of the organizational skills they wish to promote.

Personal coaching: Personal coaching is what the name infers; it is what the individual personally wants out of their life career, and how they can achieve it. The coach provides a supportive and motivating environment to explore these personal goals. The coach's role is to stimulate commitment and assist the participant toward the development of the motivation and dedication needed to achieve their goals. Performance coaching and skills coaching are often initiated by an organization. Personal coaching, or life coaching as it is also known, may be initiated by the participant themselves. Christian Life coaching incorporates biblical goals and principles into the life coaching process.

Coaching is one successful way to equip a director, pastor, teacher, coach, or manager with the tools they need, to develop the skills to lead, motivate, organize, manage and communicate.

Faith in Life Coaching

Having a Christian oriented life coaching focus, we recognize the importance of faith to produce results in any form of ministry, but especially so with life coaching.

Social scientists are prompt in exploring the significance of gender, race, and class in various endeavors of research, while often neglecting spirituality as a factor in these studies. Bender (2003) noted sociologists know remarkably little about how people practice religion in their daily activities, including work. Spirituality is often understood as highly personal, while religion is understood as "institutional, dogmatic, inflexible, and divisive". In this light, spirituality is more psychological, while religion is more sociological.

Faith has been associated with reduced work burnout and increased job satisfaction. Others argue that societies founded in religious tradition and values are more likely to resist acceptance of gender equality within their society. However, other researchers such as Rose and Brasher reveal the significance of a personal relationship with God in offering women from conservative faith traditions a source of power, freedom, and justification amid a patriarchal environment. Faith contributed to their career decisions and several administrators indicated that their faith in God was a definitive part of their calling to their career. Their perspectives seem to be more focused on praying for direction regarding the work environment, and when asked about marriage, they offered a perspective of balancing the value of their marriage with other time commitments. Some women expressed tension between balancing career and marriage commitments, but they acknowledged that faith helped provide direction in career decisions (Ponton, 1999).

Important Relationships Related to Coaching

Effective coaching requires the development of healthy relationships. Relationships are experienced as the fundamental first work of coaching and building them includes getting to know learning styles, learning personalities and differentiating the approach accordingly, and a willingness to help in informal ways. Relationships must be purposeful, a pathway to the work ahead. Establishing the coaching role and setting expectations are part of this process as well. Coaches' first interactions are marked with demonstrating and modeling, presenting oneself as "a partner," and building credibility as a fellow participant in life's journey. Healthy coaching relationships grow more comfortable, better, or deeper over time. Coaches experience most current relationships as positive or pleasant. Most students describe the coaching relationship as positive, great, awesome, or friendly. With healthy coaching, conversations become more "authentic" and "deeper". The relationships tend to be driven by a desire for professional growth, and a desire to give or receive help. Over time the mutual work provides shared experiences and positive results with students, and this builds trust and excitement. The relationships and work seem to spiral outward and upward, like a growing tree expanding in several directions simultaneously (Collins, 2009).

Time is a recurring theme for all participants. As it relates to the coaching relationship, time is required for growth. For all participants, the coaching relationships are different now than they were in the beginning. Over time anxiety subsides, and the coach observes increased self-esteem and confidence in the student. The relationship has progressed to the extent that being coached is marked with a sense of reciprocity, eagerness, and dependability. Some describe coaching as having progressed from "instructive," focused in professional literature, and about initial steps, toward more "supportive," collaborative, and collegial work. Coaching is extremely dynamic; a delicate balance of push and pull. To be coached is to be safe enough to ask any question, share any weakness and expect that the expressed need will be met respectfully. There is a strong sense of sharing and dynamic flow. Sometimes the expectations for the structure of the interactions are well established, but even when this is the case, there still tends to be an informal feel (Ellis & Bochner, 1996).

Coaching contexts and definitions are numerous. For all participants, coaching at least began with a focus in competency development. Coaching tends to have a specific focus for a period of time, and that focus is sometimes set by the student, sometimes by the coach, and sometimes by an outside correspondent. Students typically initiate coaching interactions, but sometimes coaches contact students. For the most part even when there is a specific focus, the student still sets the coaching agenda, at least in part.

Major Benefits of Coaching

Coaching is experienced as helping. Coaches help with the development of "life skills," or can focus on specific issues the coachee is facing. Coaches help find and use resources, develop overall plans, set goals, and stay focused. The coach may help with implementation, change, or completing assessments. They may help use assessments (such as the highly-recommended DISC profiles) along with other data to help make decisions about life. Coaches plan and prepare to help the coachee "move forward." About half of the participants describe what the coach does as being connected with professional growth. Coaching is designed to uplift, encourage, affirm, validate, or empower through the coaching process. Coaches model, demonstrate, and observe. Much of their work is done in a formal setting. Coaches work with students, but mostly their work is focused on improving various and necessary skills. They have conversations, many, many conversations. They provide feedback, constructive criticism, ideas, advice, or tips in ways that are "nonthreatening." Monitoring is embedded in the coaching tasks, and one coach describes evaluating even though she is not an evaluator. Coaches often collect data and monitor implementation and improvement. The metaphors that are used in describing the experiences of coaches and coaching are rich and varied. The coaching relationship was described as like a mother/father/child relationship. Another metaphor used is to see the coach as a gardener. These metaphors seem to rise from feelings of being valued and protected. Another metaphor describes the coach as a guide or a bridge to help the coachee get where they need to go. The core concept of movement and journey connect this comparison to that of the coach as guide. There is an underlying expectation that the coach has some knowledge of the journey and will be able to help the coachee navigate it more effectively and/or efficiently than he/she could alone. Another somewhat connected metaphor was the coach as a counselor. One participant used coaching, but specified a baseball or football coach. She went on to describe coaching as another tool in the toolbox to help become a better teacher. Another tool comparison was the coach as a mixer or blender. In this metaphor the coach is something extra to make things easier. Other comparisons include coach as a scaffold and a sounding board. Coaching is compared to having an extra set of hands or an extra pair of eyes. Embedded in these comparisons is the sense that the coach is practical, useful, and helpful.

The coach is an approachable and available resource to whom you can turn when you need ideas, answers, or help getting out of a rut. The experience is positive. Coaching feels relaxed, easy, and even friendly. The coach is simultaneously a peer and something more. Coaching is seen as an avenue for professional growth. Most coachees' experience friendship or friendliness between the coach and coachee. The best aspects of the coaching relationship all center on learning. For coaches the best parts are being able to observe so much good teaching, to continue learning, and to see teachers grow. From both the perspective of the coach and the one being coached, a healthy coaching relationship can and often does produce a life changing experience, for both parties involved.

Mentoring and Coaching as Leadership Tools

Difference Between Mentoring and Coaching

Coaching, and Mentoring, are not the same thing. In 1998 an online survey was conducted to define what protégés felt were the attributes of effective mentoring relationships (see http://www.coachingandmentoring.com/surveyresults.htm). A resounding YES came from responses to this open-ended question: Is there a difference between a mentor, a coach, and a supervisor?

These differences are summarized in Table 1:

Table 1: Differences between Mentoring and Coaching

	Mentor	Coach
Focus	Individual	Performance
Role	Facilitator with no agenda	Specific agenda
Relationship	Self-selecting	Comes with the job
Source of influence	Perceived value	Position
Personal returns	Affirmation/ learning	Teamwork/performance
Arena	Life	Task related

Coaches focus on a specific set of problems, or the "results of the job," exploring solutions and opportunities for the employee to use (Megginson, 1995).

The mentor, on the other hand, zeros in on the individual, focusing not only on the present, but with an eye always focused on the future. Mentors do provide some of the same services as coaches, but they are built on a complex, ever-evolving synergetic relationship that is based on mutual respect and a friendship of sorts (Megginson, 1995).

In Practice

I met Jillian through a mutual friend. At 27, she was moving up the corporate ladder of her company, while juggling her roles as wife and mother to two pre-school children. Understandably, her level of stress was high, and her hope was to learn to manage her life more efficiently.

In our first meeting, after a brief "getting to know you" time, I asked her some key questions:

- What would you say is your most important value? Her answer was her marriage and family.
- My follow up question was, "How is your present pursuit up the corporate ladder helping or hindering the achievement of living out your most important value?"

Our discussion from there opened many doors, and led to some key changes that she determined she needed to make.

"Coachable people seek out those who speak truth to them, even if it is a painful truth, because it protects them and it makes them a better person and leader."

Gary Rohrmayer

Chapter 2:
The Balanced Life Philosophy:
What is a Balanced Life?

It was way back in the last century, around 1970, that I first heard of the Balanced Life Philosophy. I was a Campus Life, Youth for Christ club member, and my director, a brother named Rich Hanson, shared this concept, rooted in Luke 2:52

> "And Jesus grew in wisdom and knowledge, and in favor with God and man."

I hope it is safe to assume that anyone you may coach will understand that Jesus was fully human and fully divine. As a human, he had to grow, as do we; thus, Jesus grew physically, mentally, socially or relationally and spiritually. All four areas are important. If Jesus had to grow, how much more do we?

It has been my observation over this past 40 plus years that a life out of balance is a life filled with difficulty and often regret, and most coaching will revolve around helping someone find health and fresh balance in one or more of these areas of life. Of course, people in general need balance and health, and leaders in family and church need it perhaps most of all.

Breaking life down into categories can help you identify a balance of goals and dreams in all areas, and minimize the tendency to forget something important. Asking questions is what coaches and mentors do, and asking key questions regarding these areas of importance can provide great insight into the person being coached. Thus, questions need to be asked in the areas of:

- <u>Physical</u>: When coaching, a person's overall health should be considered. Many psychological problems and spiritual issues can be traced to inadequate health; some caused by physical diseases such as diabetes, or severe anxiety or psychosomatic disorders, stress unmanaged can rob a person of their ability to function fully. In Western culture, appearance can make a difference in one's perceived ability and overall success, but especially appearance or lack thereof of health and vitality. Thus, be willing to ask questions related to physical health of a client, and be willing to make suggestions to better the client's health. The coach should not shy away from asking questions and making observations in the areas of health and recreation, to include hobbies, sports, fitness, diet, health care, sleep, Sabbath, vacations – the things that take care of you, physical health should not be ignored in the coaching process.

- <u>Mentally</u>: A client's mental growth goes beyond academic achievement or simple IQ. The ability to learn, adapt, communicate, evaluate and discern is essential for personal and professional growth, as is one's ability to gain insight, necessary to make effective change towards one's goals. Evaluation of a client's intellectual capabilities, education, and ability to apply knowledge to real world problems (Wisdom) must be done to avoid making false promises regarding the potential of the person you are coaching, leading to false hope. Desire and faith must be measured against human limits and reality. Though I may want and believe I can be a National Basketball star, at my age and being only 5"10" it is not likely to happen. Of course, we all have limitations, and limitations can be overcome… sometimes through hard work, additional study, more education, etc. All these things a coach will discuss with his or her coachee as a part of developing a plan of action.

- <u>Socially/Relationally</u>: It is rare, but at times I will meet a potential client whose personality, demeanor, manner or lack thereof and general social ineptitude make me want to start heavy drinking! This will not in and of itself close a door to helping them, if the person is aware of their deficits. But when someone, quite possibly well qualified, lacks social graces or is at least a semblance of emotional intelligence, it is hard to work with them. I don't care how much a person may make or what doors might open if I work with them, narcissistic people are not worth the time or energy. Of course, Jesus was able to help the seemingly helpless, as should any true follower of Jesus. Jesus was a friend of sinners…those who frequently missed the mark in life, or who were not reaching healthy goals. In fact, all his disciples had flaws, but he worked with them anyway. As a coach, we must be friendly; warm, empathic and kind, as does a coachee, or at least we hope they will grow in that direction. Relationships with friends and neighbors, plus your community service: PTA, politics, volunteering, boards, service projects, etc., along with one's family –our spouse, children and extended family relationships are all important in developing a healthy, balanced life.

- Spirituality: In my book, Journey to Wholeness[4] I identify three stages of spiritual growth, as presented by John the Apostle; children, young men and fathers. Without going into details on this teaching (hint, buy the book) all believers in Christ are on a spiritual journey, with needs to be fulfilled and tasks to complete. Spiritual growth, though innate (Christ in us; the Holy Spirit working in us), and progressive, can be thwarted by overt and un-repented sin, lack of knowledge, poor spiritual disciplines, or insufficient biblical value integration. A coach should neither neglect nor over emphasize the importance of spiritual growth, remembering that balance is a key to success in life and God's Kingdom.

More will be said on how to integrate these heart concepts with the coaching process, below, but for now, remember that balance is

---

[4] Journey to Wholeness, Dr. Stan DeKoven, www.booksbyvision.com

key, and a necessary ingredient to the abundant life Jesus promised us (John 10:10). Further, in the questionnaire used to evaluate clients are key questions to ask to find out the balance of the person you are coaching.

Finding balance and health in life is critical and a core focus in Christian Life coaching.

Five "C's" of a Healthy Leader

Many years later I met a wonderful man of God, Dr. Malcolm Weber, the creator of Vision International University's Masters in Leadership program. Malcolm introduced us to his Five C's philosophy, and with his permission, it is expounded upon as a primary foundation of our philosophy of our coaching program.

Christ

As a Christian Life Coach, there are many things we cannot do for our clients; one thing of greatest importance; is to reveal Christ to them. Some will call the revelation of Christ as the deep and abiding knowledge of the Father's love for us, in Christ by the Holy Spirit. To truly know that one is forgiven, accepted, affirmed and included in the love of the Father, Son and Spirit is foundational to living the Christian life. Jesus stated that we are to love God with our whole being (Matthew 22: 37-39) and our neighbor… which can only be done (and never perfectly) if we embrace what God has poured out; His love, on us (Romans 5:5). Thus, we can love God, only because he first loved us (1 John 4:19).

As a Christian Life Coach, we can encourage this deeper relation with the Lord, model it (if we have experienced it ourselves), and lead the client like a horse to water, but remember, we cannot make them drink… but we can pour salt in the oats so they want to drink or deepen their personal life in Christ.

For the Christian, and as a Christian leader, all of life starts and ends with **Christ**. Thus, all coaching will be centered in Christ; seeking to bring those being coached into Christ-like thinking. This requires fellowship, which is part of what we provide in the coaching setting.

During his early ministry, Jesus lived in continuous fellowship with his Father. This inward, spiritual fellowship was the source of everything in his life and ministry. A true follower will seek to follow and lead from a place of union with Christ, as Jesus' leadership came from his union with his Father. In the relationship between Jesus and his Father, we are going to find a parallel to what our own relationship with God can be.

As Paul testified: God…was pleased to reveal his Son in me…

This is the simple nature of the Christian life: union with Jesus, and living by means of his indwelling life. Thus, this is the source of Christian leadership. Jesus' disciples led out of their fellowship with him (Acts 4:13). Jesus is the vine and we are the branches. Only in him can we bear leadership-fruit that is pleasing to God.

Unfortunately, many Christian leaders are too busy with "ministry stuff" to spend sufficient time developing their inward lives in Christ. When a leader builds his inner life in Christ first, then his whole ministry will change… and a coach's responsibility is to help the coachee to establish and maintain a healthy and vibrant relationship with God our Father.

Community

The second C in our philosophy of coaching speaks of the importance of **Community** in the establishment of our relationship with Christ and the transformation of our character.

As a Christian Life Coach, you will do much more listening than talking. My dear mom told me many times, there is a reason God made you with one mouth and two ears; so, you will listen twice as much as you talk! There is wisdom in that statement indeed.

Listening takes time and energy. Our time as a coach focuses on the goals and dreams of the client. Our hope is that along with personal and professional goals being reached, that change and growth in the grace and knowledge of our Lord and Savior Jesus Christ will occur. Growth comes as various paradigms, (belief systems) are challenged in light of the word of God within community. If a client is not part of a healthy community, they need to be. Being aware of their community and helping them to establish accountability within that community is positively essential to their process of growth and change.

The Christian life is a personal union and fellowship with Jesus (John 17:3). Church life is knowing God together. Together, the community of believers can experience God in his fullness. Spiritual maturity is a corporate experience, not just an individual one. In the life of the community, as we love and serve one another, the daily realities of our own walk with Jesus are expressed in our relationships with one another.

Christian unity is not a unity of structure, but of fellowship. Christian fellowship is a heart to heart, "deep calls to deep," intimate spiritual communion. Church life is both a foretaste and a beginning of everlasting life. Leaders too, need healthy communities around them.

In these "safe environments," people have the freedom to be honest and to grow within boundaries framed by shared values and common goals.

Healthy community forms the context in which individual callings and responsibilities are expressed in order to fulfill the community's corporate purpose. In a healthy community, the individual callings work together to fulfill the community's calling.

Character

As a Christian Life Coach, we know that no one (but Jesus) is perfect. Though perfection is not required before one is qualified to minister, lead, serve, etc., maturity is. The biblical word for maturity is telios, best defined as being everything we are supposed to be at any given time. Thus, a well-functioning 8-year-old would be considered telios (mature) if he is acting like an 8 year old, where as a 35 year old man who is underemployed, struggling with relationships, not living up to his realistic potential would not be telios, but immature.

Maturity speaks about character, and healthy coaching focuses on character and strong, healthy Christian character will sustain us in the vicissitudes of life.

Building a strong **Character** is the goal of all training; not just an accumulation of knowledge. The indwelling life of Christ expressed and worked out in community, will develop godly character.

In leadership, people are not only motivated to follow a leader's captivating vision or his compelling communication skills, but also by their sense of the leader's desire to serve and his/her high integrity and consistency. Character is a "non-negotiable" requirement of a leader.

There are three essential elements of developing character: discipline, proving and accountability.[5]

Discipline:

At the heart of character lies discipline. When discipline matures, he is then permitted by God to give discipline to others. He has become a leader.

Proving:

A leader does not become one overnight. He must be tested first (1 Timothy 3:10). He must undergo the preparations of God. This goes against our culture, which wants instant success. We want to start at "the top," but that is not the way of God.

Accountability is the Key. Healthy leaders will always be accountable!

---

[5] My thanks to the seminal work on the 5 C's done by Dr. Malcolm Webber, http://www.strategicpress.org/

Character is not just what a person will ideally be in the future. Character is what a person is at this present time. It is not only how a person acts. It also includes a person's inner thoughts, motives and attitudes. A person's character is not revealed without pressure. Character is not only that which other people see on the external. It is what other people do not see. Character is not limited to having the wisdom to comment on the behavior of others.

To a man of character, God can entrust a calling.

Calling

Over the past 10 years, I have tried to coach a handful of folks who, on the surface, appeared to have "all the right stuff" for ministry success; but they did not. Nor did they have a humble (clear and accurate) appraisal of themselves. Frankly, they were full of themselves, felt above everyone else, and were thus unteachable. Sad really.

In Coaching, there are times where one must concede that the greatest amount of faith and skill will not produce the dream (fantasy) of the coachee. Being a mirror of reality can be hard, and one must have sensitivity and grace, and be open to the impossible… but sometimes, no matter how hard you try, it just won't work… they lack the calling to be who they are dreaming they will be.

One way to help a client is to ask questions leading to an honest appraisal of their calling and gifts. It is more loving to disappoint a client than to see them crash and burn because they did not have what it takes to achieve their goal… but one caution.

Dead Arm Doris

In my senior year of high school, in the last century, I visited my guidance counselor. She was a stern lady with a withered arm, a birth defect I was told. She was known around schools as a woman who was rather unsympathetic (harsh) in style. I was inquiring about college, as my ambition was to go to college, become a counselor and minister, etc. She looked at my grades and pronounced "not a chance", then asked me a question. "What does your father do for a living?" I told her he worked for the United States Postal Service as a truck driver. She responded "you should forget about college and see if your dad can get you a job at the Post Office... you will never make it in University."

Well, I left our "coaching session" more than angry, determined to prove her wrong. In fact, I vowed to send her a copy of my Ph.D. diploma when I graduated just to show her how wrong she was. Of course, by the time I had finished my degree her opinion no longer mattered. Her coaching could easily have discouraged me to a point of quitting the pursuit of my dream... but thank God I had a genuine call on my life that could not be stolen by unwise counsel.

A person's **Calling** can be observed, developed, and proven within the immediate context of the community.

A leader must have a calling and a vision from God or else he would be wise not to lead (James 3:1). A true calling comes from God. Then it becomes the leader's own vision; something she can share passionately with others. Strong calling must not be disconnected from a deep surrender to and relationship with Christ. Christ comes first! In addition, the calling must be submitted to community.

Today, man-appointed leaders look upon spiritual leadership as a profession or a career. They are more concerned with the medical benefits or retirement accounts that come with the "job" than they are for the sheep of God. They are the "hired hands" (John 10:12-13).

True leadership will be appointed by God.

One's individual calling will be the result of a very complex interaction between the following elements in the leader's life, including personality, culture, gender, age, physical condition, leader/manager orientation, genes, life expectations, relationships, role models, mentors, family heritage, current family, spiritual gifts, motivational gifts, ministry gifts, formal education and training experiences.

Thus, there are not only five callings (e.g., Ephesians 4) but an almost infinite number of callings that match everyone perfectly in the purposes of God.

A divine calling to lead, establishes the leader's purpose, passion and commission.

Purpose

Leaders must have a clear purpose for their leadership and this purpose must be established by God. Without a clear understanding of his purpose, the leader will not accomplish much.

Having a clear understanding of his calling will allow the leader to focus and be more effective (e.g., Exodus 18:13-26; 2 Corinthians 10:13-18).

Passion

Leadership is risky work. The way is frequently hard (Acts 14:22); only the truly committed will make it.

Only those who can passionately communicate the exciting possibilities of the future will be able to persuade others to follow them down a frequently difficult path.

Commission

In the leader's life, there will be a specific time of divine commission when he or she is set apart for the work to which God has called him.

This commission was given by the Holy Spirit (Acts 13:4; cf. Matthew 9:38; 1 Corinthians 1:1; Galatians 1:1; Deuteronomy 31:14) in the context of the authority/structure of the church ("they placed their hands on them and sent them off", Acts 13:3; cf. Acts 6:3-6).

The commission comes at a certain time and constitutes the leader's "marching orders." Thus, the calling comes from God and is then confirmed by the community.

Here is where some emerging leaders err. They know that God has called them to a certain ministry and they function to some extent in gifts associated with that ministry. But they err when they begin to assume they have the authority of that ministry before they are actually commissioned.

Authority does not come from gifting; it comes from the commission. As you are faithful in what he gives you to do, God might expand your field of ministry (Luke 16:10). Paul faithfully taught for years before receiving his apostolic commission.

Competence

I love to sing, and am told I do it well. I have always wanted to play an instrument well enough to accompany myself or lead worship. I have and do lead worship by voice (where I am competent), but would not dare try to lead with a guitar (which I can strum, but not well). I can only adequately serve in the areas of my competence.

Of course, I could, at least possibly, put in the sufficient time and energy to become more skilled with the guitar; the question becomes is it a priority, am I willing to discipline myself and invest my stewardship in the task to become competent. Much of coaching is designed to help the client determine where and how, or even how much of his or her energy will be invested in becoming competent enough to fulfill a purpose.

So how is competency developed? Competency in a particular area of life and ministry is developed and nurtured in the environment of a loving community. Competency is demonstrated by practical, hands-on training in the immediate context of the local church and community.

This is where many Christian leaders fail. They have a good knowledge of the Bible, but they have never learned how to lead people or manage the practical aspects of an organization.

Other leaders do have good strategic and technical abilities to lead, but they lack sound biblical knowledge.

Paul told Timothy to choose elders who had some basic organizational competencies. (1 Timothy 3:4-5). This was in contrast to the false leaders at Ephesus who did not know what they were doing. (1 Timothy 1:7). Thus, the leader must "know how" to do it.

It is absolutely necessary that a leader have strong competencies. There are many kinds of competencies that are necessary for the leaders to have. Essentially, the individual's calling defines his necessary competencies

Competence is the last part of our model of a healthy leader.

Conclusion

At the end of this work I will discuss a concept crystalized by Ken Blanchard and his team in his book ***Collaboration Begins with You: Be a Silo Buster*** by Berrett-Koehler Publishers. In the book, he presents the idea of collaboration as a key to effective leadership, and that would certainly be true in coaching. It is indeed a collaborative effort between the coach and his student or client. In Dr. Blanchard's book he uses the analogy of balance, using the metaphor of head, heart and hands. What has been presented above is the Heart of the matter in coaching… our goal is health, wholeness; dreaming dreams and achieving worthy goals. A right heart is essential, the most important part of coaching (or life in general). In the next chapter we will look more at the heart, but start to look at the head, the necessary information and the ability to gather it well to assist the coachee to move forward towards his or her goals.

*See page 113 if you can't wait!

"Not everyone comes from a happy or functional home...and there are many wonderful stories of men and women who have overcome incredible obstacles. But what a blessing for those who have had two strong, committed and loving parents who have done their best to raise a child to maturity...it makes an incredible difference."

Dr. Stan DeKoven

40

Chapter 3:
Healthy Functional Family System

After reading the last chapter, you might be asking yourself the question, "What does this have to do with coaching?" From my perspective, everything. Our goal is to help our coachees grow, change, develop, and mature, all in the direction of health. As you will see later in this chapter, we will tie together our philosophy and the development of a healthy functional life plan.

Thus, it has been said by many that coaching is similar to parenting; especially parenting a teen. Healthy parents know that a teen must be treated differently than a child. For a child, do as I say because I said so works...but for a teen, why and how, etc., are also important. Parents learn to ask the right questions, and negotiate for solutions. The coaches/parents hope is that by the defined time (18 years for parents, whenever for coaches) that certain clearly defined goals will have been reached, and that health and function will be seen in the life of the teen/young adult. With that in mind, it is helpful to first define what a healthy and functional family looks like, and by way of contrast, a dysfunctional or unhealthy system. Of course, everyone shares, to one degree or another, aspects of both healthy and unhealthy family systems, so keep that in mind as you review this material.

Definition

A healthy functional family is one where there is an interactive, unconditionally loving, supportive environment in which all the members are individually affirmed (though not mistake free) and all the relationships between the members are functionally effective. There are several important characteristics of a healthy family. They include the following.

There is a healthy **wholeness** to the family. The family as a whole is greater than the sum of its parts, and there is a commitment to this wholeness by each member.

Families have unique personalities which can be described both positively and negatively, just as an individual can be. Family personalities can be described as close, distant, affectionate, critical, fragmented, caring, uncaring, addictive, abusive, unemotional, cold, warm, loving, unloving, controlling, angry, perfectionistic, etc. A healthy family is one with more of the positive than negative characteristics being seen.

Secondly, healthy relationships are probably the leading characteristic of a healthy, functional family system. Thus, you will find a healthy (not perfect, no such animal) marriage is modeled. In a healthy marriage, good communication between all family members is modeled, with recognition of human frailty and weakness. Perfectionism is not expected nor encouraged. Further, the family has healthy boundaries, and though perfect unconditional love is only found in God, they work towards unconditional love towards each other, while showing trust, respect and understanding.

Conflicts, which are inevitable in any relationship, are resolved through good modeling and communication skills. There is nothing wrong with conflict as long as it is clean and fair. This will mean that the following will be present:

- Right timing - there is a time and place for dealing with conflict. Again, boundaries are respected.
- Active listening versus character assassination is used in communication.
- Appropriate expression of feelings is used, without verbal or physical aggression; they learn to be assertive but not aggressive.
- Communication is in the here and now - no digging into the past or Sandbagging.

- Arguments are concrete and specific, and avoid lecturing and nagging, or withdrawing in silence or stomping out in anger.
- No global statements ('You always' and 'You never', etc.) are used, and the focus is on 'I' messages, and not 'You' or 'We' statements. Communication is honest and open, dealing with one thing at a time without arguing details (nit picking).
- The family members will be tenacious, hanging in there until the issue is resolved, while extending forgiveness when necessary.

Other primary characteristics of a healthy family are consistency and predictability in the home, with positive time spent together to express appreciation (affirmation) to each other. Also, the children are trained to take responsibility for their thoughts, feelings and actions and to honor their parents. Thus, the entire family, not just mom, has the ability and willingness to subordinate personal needs for the family needs.

Thus, the healthy family can be described as an open system, which is flexible and open to input and therefore able to change and grow over time. An open system seeks out new information designed to improve the family, and is not afraid to bring family secrets into the light. Family secrets, destructive behaviors, beliefs, rules, and myths are challenged, including challenging assumptions of previous generations, so that necessary change will occur.

Roles are clearly and healthily defined but are not rigid.

Of course, every family has rules (usually unspoken) in order to function. In a healthy family the rules will be healthy and will include:

- Appropriate expression and sharing of emotions, especially anger.
- Healthy attitudes, roles, and appropriate behavior.

- Open and honest communication, along with consistent and fair discipline.

When a family is functioning in a healthy fashion, basic human needs are met. This will mean there will be provision for the following.

- Security, self-worth and significance
- Productivity
- Challenge
- Intimacy
- Personal happiness

In a healthy family, individuality versus sameness or group compliance is valued.

The home will provide an atmosphere where family members will grow into a healthy identity. Each member will develop his or her own individuality. There will be no enmeshment (overly close) on one hand and no disengagement (emotional cut-off) on the other, but rather a constant moving towards interdependence.

Thus, the parents encourage that their children's individuality be respected. This is demonstrated by having a healthy balance between nurturing the children in the ways of the Lord while respecting their individuality.

Family therapist Virginia Satir refers to these as The Five Freedoms

- To see and hear (perceive)
- To think
- To feel
- To desire
- To imagine their own destiny (create, vision, dream)

The five freedoms are encouraged in healthy families.

There is a strong spiritual component in healthy families, where all family members are nurtured through teaching and modeling at home and church. The parents will model spiritual intimacy (oneness in the things of God). The parents will also ensure that the home is Christ-centered.

A Coaches Perspective

It has been a great blessing to conduct marriage enrichment and parenting seminars on 6 Continents. My books are used in many nations to equip ministers and help families. It used to bother me, and as I talked with Pastors of local churches, we both believed that attendance should be much higher at a seminar or workshop. We often stated "if only the ones who truly needed the seminar had shown up, how much better it could be." Well, as some say, it is what it is.

In reality, it is usually the healthier and those wanting to improve their health that…

- Join a gym
- Start a healthy eating plan
- Go back to school
- Go to enrichment seminars
- Seek counseling or coaching

Most folks you coach will be sufficiently healthy, much due to some healthy parenting or good substitutes, and they will likely benefit from coaching. If not send them to a reputable therapist to help them get healthy, and then start coaching for growth.

Thus, a healthy family is highly desirable, in spite the fact that nearly 70% of folks, and most of the ones you will coach, have come from less than ideal (healthy or functional) homes. The goal, regardless the background, is to help the coachee to achieve goals leading to health.

Before tying together our heart focus and providing some helps to utilize the concepts, it will be necessary, for sake of a rounded study, to review the characteristics of a dysfunctional family... for you are just as likely, as a coach, to work with functional and dysfunctional, and frankly, probably a bit of both in everyone you coach.

"Our parents were our first gods. If parents are loving, nurturing, and kind, this becomes the child's definition of the creator. If parents were controlling, angry, and manipulative, then this becomes their definition."

David W. Earle

48

Chapter 4:
Dysfunctional Family System

Without doubt, this author was raised in a very dysfunctional home. My parents were, like most parents, rookies at best when it came to parenting. They did their best, given who they were and the family they were raised in... and I am blessed to have had two parents, as nutty as they were at times, in my life.

Many of my previous books related to counseling have used illustrations from my life experience to present principles of God's grace and transforming power. I am fairly acquainted with dysfunction. However, it is one thing to be aware; it is another to see dysfunction in every family interaction. Learning about dysfunctional life patterns can help us know when significant obstacles may stand in the way of the coachees' potential. Dwelling on them, or searching for them is the stuff of therapy, but not of coaching.

Definition

In a dysfunctional family, the characteristics of a healthy functional family are absent or lacking. This creates levels of anxiety in all family members.

The two main components of a dysfunctional family are childhood abuse (or neglect, rejections, abandonment and betrayal) and shame. These frequently occur under the umbrella of religiosity. Harshness, legalism, rigidity and restriction often arise in the way biblical injunctions are interpreted and followed.

A dysfunctional family is one with an impaired capacity for interaction in which all members are individually ineffective in varying degrees and all the relationships between the members are functionally impaired.

The first dysfunctional family is the first family recorded in the Bible, that of Adam and Eve. This is recorded in Genesis immediately after the fall. In this family fear, blame, mistrust, rejection, shame, bitterness and murder prevailed. [6]

Few if any families presented in the Bible would be considered healthy and fully functional - all are dysfunctional. In fact, families of the great patriarchs were highly dysfunctional.

We can therefore assume that all families are dysfunctional to a degree. None are perfectly functional.

Four types of dysfunctional families have been described.

- The low achieving family.
- The perfectionist family (that expects too much).
- The preoccupied family (emotional, mental, or physical).
- The family with unfinished business (emotional issues passed down from previous generation).

Characteristics of the Dysfunctional Family

As with a healthy family, it starts with the marriage. An unhealthy marriage relationship is the foundation for an unhealthy family.

An unhealthy marriage relationship will be modeled in the following manner.

- Bonding out of need occurs rather than in a strong covenant.
- Power struggles are common, starting with family of origin, traditions, etc.

---

[6] For insight into dysfunctional patterns found in scripture, see my book *I Want to Be Like You, Dad: Breaking Free from Generational Patterns,* Vision Publishing, www.booksbyvision.com

- Enmeshment or fusion rather than differentiation is how the relationship is established and maintained.
- Thus, the parents are unable to give to children what they don't have themselves.

In the dysfunctional family, relationships suffer according to the degree of dysfunction. This is caused by...

- Poor communication with all family members.
- Boundaries are vague, obscure and fused.
- Members are either too close (enmeshment, fusion) or too distant (disengagement).

In a dysfunctional family, there is disrespect between the members in the family because:

- Intimacy is not understood.
- Conflicts cannot be properly resolved.
- Criticism of family members is common.
- Children dishonor parents.
- Selfishness and instant gratification are the order of the day.

Unhealthy patterns from previous generations are allowed to continue to affect the current family. These include the sins of the fathers, traditions, and bondages. What has been accomplished on the cross has to be appropriated to stop passing on the dysfunction.

Dysfunctional families are shrouded in varying degrees of shame. Shame is simply a result of original sin. It involves the rejection of self as being fundamentally bad, unworthy, inadequate, defective, and insufficient as a person. It is self-rejection and hatred. Shame becomes internalized, the self is abandoned and identity is lost. A false self becomes a substitute for the real self.

The origin and perpetuation of shame can be from the following:

- External traumatic shaming events (abuse, addictions, etc.)
- Inherited generational shame (secrets and myths)
- Maintained shame (shame begets shame, abuse attracts abuse)

A shame-bound family is a group of people, all of who feel hurt and alone together. Characteristics of a shame-bound family include the following.

- Loneliness and brittle relationships.
- Denial.
- Secrecy
- Resistance to change.
- Vague and distorted boundaries.
- Perfectionism.

For many shame-based persons the biggest problem occurs in regards to boundaries. It has been helpfully said that boundaries are like a zipper. Most people are able to control the zipper from the inside. They limit other people's access to themselves and maintain their self-respect. If somebody wants something, they are able to say No and risk disapproval. Shame-based people have their zipper on the outside where anybody can have access to it. They find it difficult to say, 'No'.

Shame families have many masks, to conceal the shame and suppress feelings. They include:

- The Analytical family (analyzing to explain away the pain)
- Fairy-tale family (pretense, fantasy, imitation).
- Blaming family (a scapegoat is found inside or outside the family).
- Disconnected family (isolated, whole family or part of it).

- Survival of the Fittest Family (rough and tough).
- Nice family (sickly-sweet, sacrifice, religiosity).

In dysfunctional families, there is often a denial of the child's individuality, which interferes with the child's freedom to perceive, think, feel, desire, and create.

Claudia Black describes the dysfunctional family roles. These appear according to the degree of dysfunction. They include:

- Primary Dysfunctional Person (abuser, addict, handicapped, chronically ill, etc.), he or she has a root problem of pain and shame.
- Primary Enabler, who tries to make everything look good (usually the spouse); they have a root problem of hurt and anger.
- Hero Child - the super-responsible one and perfectionist, who think that by being perfect problems will go away, usually the eldest child. He has a root problem of inadequacy and guilt.
- Scapegoat – the irresponsible one or family rebel, and the one who gets the blame for the family dysfunction; he has a root problem of hurt and anger.
- Clown (or Mascot) – the placater who performs to cover up family dysfunction. He has a root problem of insecurity and fear.
- Lost Child – the adjuster, loner and dreamer; He has a root problem of rejection, anger and fear. This is often the youngest child.

There are other roles played by an enabler in the family, such as martyr, messiah, caretaker, rescuer, persecutor and victim.

Rigid rules will also be present in a dysfunctional family system. With this comes authoritarianism. Any degree of flexibility will not be tolerated.

When two family members cannot normally resolve conflict, there is a build-up of anxiety and a third person is triangulated in, to ease the anxiety. Many such triangles may exist in a family. The classical triangle is that of persecutor, victim and rescuer. An unhealthy secret coalition is formed between the victim and rescuer.

Perfectionism is common in the dysfunctional family, and even more so in Christian families who try to maintain an acceptable church standard.

Unhealthy family secrets will be present in a dysfunctional family. These are things that are not spoken about because of family shame. They are covered up. It may be a suicide, an illicit relationship, an illegitimate child, a criminal behavior, a serious addiction, or the like.

Scripture refers to, the hidden things of shame (2 Corinthians 4:2, Ephesians 5; 8-12). While these secrets are maintained the family dysfunction will also remain.

The dysfunctional family is characterized by degrees of inconsistency and unreliability. A highly dysfunctional person or family is consistently inconsistent.

Everyone in a dysfunctional family has varying degrees of unhealthy people dependency, and in addition, often other dependency problems. A dysfunctional family is one that functions in pain. Abandonment and shame produces pain. There is frequent unclean and dirty fighting; it is the opposite to clean and fair fighting, and involves:

- Poor listening.
- Many You and We statements.
- Many global statements (You always, You never).
- Withdrawing in anger or silence.
- Dragging up the past and being suspicious.

- Passive/aggressive behavior - subtle indirect anger, teasing, forgetting, difficult.
- Procrastinating, being difficult, uncooperative.
- Labeling - such as paranoid, co-dependent, inadequate, stupid.
- Condescending - giving in, tactical retreat.
- Brutal frankness - insensitive to feelings.
- Children triangled as a weapon.
- Sex used as a weapon.
- Childhood Abuse.

As a coach, you will undoubtedly encounter many people with both functional and dysfunctional patterns. Be aware of this. If you are coaching someone that is more dysfunctional than functional, you might consider making a referral to a trained mental health professional, unless you are dually trained to handle coaching and therapy... know your limitations and keep healthy boundaries in your practice.

Tying it Together

In coaching, similar to counseling or mentoring, knowing the heart of the matter is vital. Whether a coach, counselor or mentor, listening to the story of the heart of the person you are coaching is your first and foremost focus. Thus, whether I use formal or informal tools to assess the heart of a person, I keep these three things in mind:

- What is the foundation of their life... are they living a fairly balanced life, and are they growing in all areas?
- Are they working towards being a healthy person, whether starting out functionally or not and are they health conscious, and striving to achieve optimal health for themselves, in their family, work, etc.?

- Are they becoming, by God's grace, a healthy leader, where Christ is first in their life, living in a committed community, with strong ethical character, understanding their calling and competent in what they do? (Remember the 5 C's)

Finally, in Proverbs 4:7 we read;

> "The beginning of wisdom is: Acquire wisdom; and with all your acquiring, get understanding."

The goal in life of a man or woman in ancient Israel was neither fame nor fortune, but the development of a wise lifestyle, which required the gathering of knowledge and understanding applied to life. This requires hard work, diligent effort, and faith or trust in a mentor/coach to help you towards this most noble life goal… wisdom.

This is the heart of the matter!

"Great Leaders develop through a never ending process of self-study, self-reflection, education, training, and experience."

Tony Buon,
The Leadership Coach: A Teach Yourself Personal Guide to Success

Chapter 5:
The Head: Understanding Style...and the Art of Communication

Introduction

One of the most important coaching functions begins when we make a meaningful/accurate assessment of the needs of the client in the effort to provide healthy coaching guidance. For the highly gifted and skilled coach, with many years of experience, assessment may be natural and more informal. However, for the novice or even a relatively new coach, tools for assessment that provide useful information... and make you look and sound like the expert you are becoming are necessary and a great advantage.

One tool that I have found most helpful, and one that is emphasized here, is the DISC profile. Especially in a 360-degree view of a client, the information obtained in this fairly quick screening device can be a powerful addition to your coaching portfolio.

Have you ever wished that everyone else thought and acted the way you do? Do you wonder why they actually do what they do? Church leaders, especially pastors, have told me they have actually thought "Church life would be great...if it weren't for all the PEOPLE issues!" This is a huge point. On a personal note, it was a subtle-but-profound realization that NOT EVERYBODY thought or processed information like me. I did NOT realize that I had unwittingly projected my own way(s) of thinking on others. SO... I assumed that everyone wanted what I wanted, and I coached, counseled, and influenced without a clear understanding of the individual.

Understanding people is a lot easier once you have a few clues on how to "read them." This part of the book is all about the dynamics of DISC- an important element of our emotional intelligence (EQ). The more "People-Smart" you are, the higher your Emotional

Quotient, and therefore the greater your success can be, in relationships.

Since everything in church life, and in the life in the marketplace, is a function of relationships, developing skills and confidence in our own self-understanding is a crucial starting point. Then our ability to "people read" are keys to getting the results we want and ultimately in helping others achieve their God given potential.

History of DISC

The development of DISC is attributed to William Marston, PhD who set out to examine observable "normal" behavior in a particular environment. Marston left behind a vast legacy across several disciplines. A lawyer, psychologist and author or co-author of several books and articles, many have come to know Marston for his work on the systolic blood pressure test that led to the invention of the polygraph. Others recognize him as the creator of the Wonder Woman comic and a champion of women's causes.

Marston graduated from doctoral studies at Harvard in the newly developing field of psychology. His landmark book, 'Emotions of Normal People', published in 1928 showcased his extensive research and theory behind the DISC model. He found that behavioral characteristics can be grouped together in four main divisions called personality styles. People with similar styles tend to exhibit specific behavioral characteristics common to that style. Marston named four dimensions of behavior, and created a means to identify the relative propensity of individuals to behave accordingly. The acronym DISC is represented by:

- **D (Drive):** Direct, Decisive, High ego strength, Problem solver, Risk taker, Self-starter (I like the term "Starter")

- **I (Influence):** Enthusiastic, Trusting, Optimistic, Persuasive, Talkative, Impulsive, Emotional (I like the term "Promoter")

- **S (Steadiness):** Good listener, Team player, Possessive, Steady, Predictable, Understanding (I like the term "Finisher")

- **C (Compliance):** Accurate, Analytical, Conscientious, Fact-finder, Systematic, High standards (I like the term "Upholder")

For the most part, there are no pure styles, but all people share these four styles in varying degrees of intensity represented by graphs with a midline. These composite styles are known as style blends, each with their own characteristics, preferences, fears, strengths and limitations.

Fast forward to the present and this system has become known as the universal language of behavior because of its simplicity and sincerity. The language is easily learned, understood, and administered by widespread audiences. Since it has been established, DISC has consistently proven to be a reliable, valid, and legally-defensible instrument for Human Resources (HR), managing, filtering, hiring, coaching, consulting, training, counseling, and countless other fields and functions.

What is DISC?

The DISC Personality System is the universal language of communication - behavior. Research has shown that behavioral characteristics can be grouped together in four major divisions called personality styles. To reiterate, people with similar styles tend to exhibit specific behavioral characteristics common to that style. All people share these four styles in varying degrees of intensity. The acronym DISC stands for the four personality styles represented by the letters:

- D (Drive)
- I (Influence)
- S (Steadiness)
- C (Compliance)

Why Do We Do What We Do?

Why are people so predictable? Why do some people drive you crazy? How is it that once you understand a person's style and what is important to them, everything else about them seems to makes sense?

When we know another person's Personality, Needs, and Motivated Styles, we can reduce or eliminate the challenges that we experience when we work with those who do not think and act as we do. Successful coaching begins with understanding the communication style and motivation of your coachee. DISC helps you do so.

It is a matter of finding out exactly what others want. The bottom line is, all people want, to be loved, valued, acknowledged, and accepted just the way they are; and the way they are not. Thus, people with a Behavioral Profile that is dominated by....

> D's, want to be valued/appreciated/acknowledged.
>
> I's, want to be loved/exalted/pointed at/worshipped.
>
> S's, want to be included/considered/given feedback
>
> C's, want their thought processes to be understood and their priorities agreed with.

After all, we are our own favorite subjects. Most people want to be seen for the strengths of their personality, and they would rather we ignore their weaknesses. We hate being told we have to change any part of how we are. Yet we spend thousands of dollars in trying to change ourselves, trying to "improve."

Want the good news? Well, you don't have to change anything! The way you are naturally, is just fine. It is certainly one POSSIBLE way of being. So what is it you want to change? And why?

- You want better relationships?

- You'd like to be able to provide better service to your church?
- You would like to be a better team player?
- You want to know who to recruit, to make a "winning team?'
- You want to consistently reach your personal goals?

If we listened to the advice of everyone else that tried to change us, we might think there was NOTHING right with us and that EVERYTHING we did was wrong! The truth is; sometimes what we do, and how we do what we do, doesn't work for others around us or for the role we are taking on. When other people speak up about it, they are only reflecting the "truth" as they see it; through their own eyes and style preferences.

So, if we want to get along with others, to have better relationships, to build a better team, to touch more people for God, we better get to know ourselves as thoroughly as possible. Then we can make better choices or make the appropriate changes in our own styles at the appropriate time with the appropriate types of people.

Make sense? It is simple when you know the rules of the game with people. And it all comes down to style. But how do we do that? How can we understand ourselves and others better? How do we get from where we are to where we want to be?

Here's the catch! To get to where you are going, you have to know from where you have started!

Where Are You Coming From?

In other words, it is easier to learn how to get somewhere when we know from where we are starting! This is why we use the DISC Profile System. It provides a point of departure-where you were, and where you are right now, - a virtual "snapshot" of how you act - at least where you see yourself right now.

It only takes a few minutes to complete a profile, but the results are amazingly accurate - if you are honest in your answers and if you reflect on how you are when you are successful, having fun or knowing you are doing a great job. (If you haven't had a profile done lately, please go to www.vision.edu/DISC)

Your DISC Profile is ideally done every six months, because you are constantly changing and if is wise to measure your progress and see how you have been adapting. Your Report is a multi-page blueprint that can help you and others understand who you are, from a behavioral point of view. It shows where you are starting from, where you see yourself today, and is the first step in helping to guide you to where you want to be.

The Windows of Our Self: The Johari Window

Let's examine what is going on - all the time - in the background of our lives as we move in and out of our daily activities and relationships with others - both at work and at home.

In every relationship, we have areas of open familiarity, and other areas that are closed off to some. Our areas of 'openness' and 'closedness' slide open and shut like four panes in a window.

A popular way to describing this is referred to as the "Johari Window" - a training model that came from the work of Joseph Luft and Harry Ingham, two training consultants who created it for their work with group processes.

According to this model, the human personality consists of four parts - four "windows" (see diagram). The terms for the windows describe types of information and who has access to it. We can use the Johari Window as an analogy of the degree to which we share, give or receive feedback. It allows people to understand themselves better, and to see how open they are to feedback given by other people. It is a moving, flexible, four-section 'window" that helps the person map out the different aspects of themselves in the following categories:

The Johari Window

	Known to Self	Unknown to Self	
	Public Area	Blind Area	Known to Others
	Hidden Area	Unknown Area	Unknown to Others

Feedback from Others (top); Disclosure to Self (left)

The first area is the Public Area or Arena. These are the things both you and other people know about you. These things are public information and are also obvious to you. With feedback from others and a lot of sharing with others, the arena would be large in proportion to other areas.

The second area is the facade or Mask. These are things that you know about yourself, but that others don't know about you. Telling people more about you can reduce the facade.

The third area is the Blind Spot. These are things that others know about you, but of which you may not be aware. Asking people for more feedback can reduce the blind spot.

The fourth area is the Unknown or Potential, as neither you nor others are aware of them. Some of the things in this area can be reached by more feedback or more disclosure among people; group interaction often brings up old memories and experiences that were "forgotten." However, there will always be some unknown and secret area in all of us.

What happens when we change our behaviors in any one of the areas?

In a good team, everyone communicates so most of the information lands in the "Public Window" or Arena.

A decrease of the Blind Area occurs when the individual receives feedback from others.

A decrease of the Hidden area occurs when the individual discloses himself/herself to others.

Unexpected insights may reduce the Unknown area.

The more authentic one becomes, the larger the Public area/Arena is, and the more open the behavior. New, conscious openness replaces former shyness and fear.

To see where you operate most often, you might want to create an intuitive map of your own Johari window. Think about yourself and ask yourself if you have a large Arena or Facade. Give some general proportions to your own window, and consider what it indicates about the public and private aspects of your life.

If you have a large Unknown/Potential area, this offers you the least potential for self-awareness, since you are not accustomed to many interactions about yourself with others. Similarly, a large Arena offers great potential for self-awareness and reflects the open sharing and receiving of feedback you have allowed in the past.

The panes in this window are not static. The general proportions of your windows will change with time, depending upon your actions. As you share more information with people, both the Facade and the Unknown decrease. As you receive more feedback from people, the Blind Spot and the Unknown decrease.

To get different results, we need different actions. Let's see what actions and attitudes each area suggests:

Arena	Blind Spot
Open and attentive	"Bull in China Shop"
(Gives and takes feedback)	(Gives, but does not take feedback)
Facade	Unknown
Interviewer style	Turtle
(Takes - does not give feedback)	(Does not give or take feedback)

The goal of soliciting feedback and self-disclosure is to move the proportions of your map so that the arena is larger - to make you more self-aware as you become more open, you essentially examine your life. The arena type of self-awareness is useful to the individual alone, but is also perceived by groups of people as open and above-board attitude, and arena type behavior is rarely misinterpreted.

Ask yourself...

In which window do I spend most of my time? And with whom?

Would opening or closing any of these windows with a certain person make a difference in the quality of my relationships? How might I do this?

How are my relationships with people in general?

Write down or have a discussion with someone about your answers, and what is possible because of these actions. Talk about which windows you are in and whether that is OK or not with other people you are in relationship with. Design more of what works for both of you. You might consider the following!

I interact with others most often from the _____ window.

I think this is because_____

In the past, it served me to do this because_____

Presently it serves me because_____

In the future I think I will spend more time in the _____ parts of the Johari Window because_____

With knowledge gained from self-examination, let's analyze all the different ways people behave so we can learn more about ourselves and appreciate others more too. This is one of the gifts of a DISC profile

To gain self-understanding, picture a personality as having four potentially equal parts. All of our possible personal characteristics are found in these four parts and we spend time in all four of them during the day. Overall, however, we tend to spend more time in one area of the circle. Which is it for you?

In each of our actions involving another person, we draw from these personality characteristics as we respond to particular situations. Use this model to help you determine where you are, and where another person you are interacting with might be.

The DISC for Self and Other Awareness

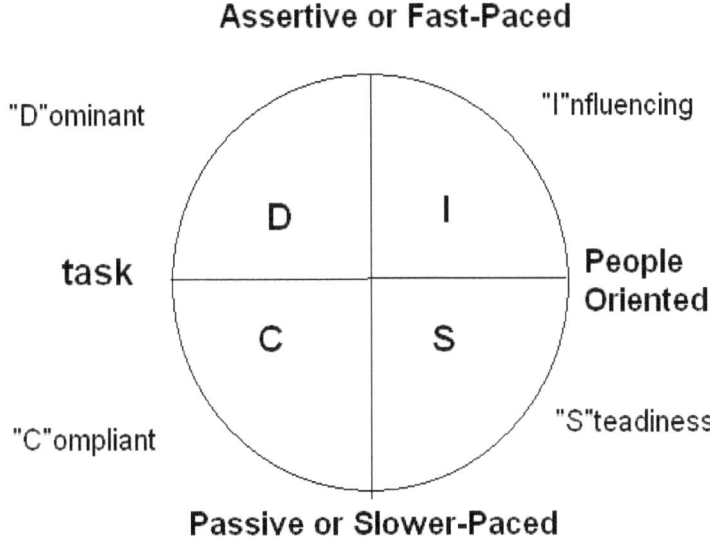

To determine the overall style of anyone you are with, watch their behavior for a few minutes and then answer the following questions.

Are they more ACTIVE or PASSIVE? (Outgoing, friendly, big picture, strong ego?)

Are they TASK ORIENTED or PEOPLE ORIENTED? (Focuses on things or people?) With the appropriate answer, you will get their style.... which is important, as we will see, in effective communication.

Why Do I Do What I Do?

Here's the key to DISC understanding. When we spend time in one part of the model more than others, it is because we have NEEDS that drive us to stay there. This determines our behavior.

D's

When we are in the D quadrant, our "D"OMINANT style characteristics are "high". We need to assertively and swiftly deal with Problems and Tasks. When our "D" is high, we act decisively, making quick decisions. We can be competitive, blunt, outspoken, restless, aggressive or defiant.

Our "D"OMINANT style characteristics are "low" when we are more calculating, mild, unassuming, deliberate, and cautious. We confront problems more thoughtfully. Where High D's have a high NEED to be in control, Low "D's do not. Low D's take on more qualities of their opposite style - High S - when it comes to meeting problems. They are patient and they politely wait their turn to speak.

I's

Next is our influencing characteristic - I style. When we do what we do using this part of our personality, we have a need to be with people — we are actively friendly, outgoing, relaxed and optimistic. We talk a lot and we are willing to be flexible, always taking others' thoughts (about us) into consideration.

When our I dimension is lower, we tend to be more like our opposite - High C - more pessimistic, factual, logical objective and aloof about people. We have little need for social approval like the High I's.

S's

When in the S quadrant, our S characteristics are high in intensity and we slow way down, meeting a need for stability or steadiness. We feel that emotional control is very important, so we rarely show our feelings. Patience is our greatest strength. A moderate pace is best. Seriousness is valuable. Our actions are deliberate. We stay organized and happy.

When we act from Low S needs, we are much more willing to share feelings. We are restless, impatient, eager, alert, mobile and discontent with the status quo — more like the High D's in energy, in terms of the need for the pace of our environment.

C's

The fourth section includes our C - Compliance behavior. The C style includes more passive actions that seek competence. We are concerned with precision, accuracy, complying with the rules and regulations. We are cautious, calculating, well-disciplined and logical. We are cautious when making decisions.

And when our C "need" is low, we share with our opposite High I's little need for rules; rather we prefer to make up our own as the situation warrants it... and in our viewpoint, that is almost always!

Where Does Our Style Come From?

Our basic orientation towards life is a combination of nature (our genes) and nurture; our parents, education, culture, etc. Both play a part. Primarily, our personal behavioral style has developed through the feedback we have received from other people. When we act in certain ways, other people respond — either positively or negatively (it totally depends on what style the OTHER person is!).

The "Voices of Authority" - parents, grandparents, aunts, uncles, church leaders, teachers and older siblings, in our life all helped shape our personality, by telling us what they liked and what they did not like about our personality.

If we got lots of negative responses from people we tended to drop those negative behaviors. Conversely, the actions that pleased others helped us to feel good or achieve results; they tended to strengthen or support our style. The development of our behavioral style begins with:

1. BELIEFS

2. ATTITUDES

3. ACTIONS

4. RESULTS

Let's review each briefly here.

Beliefs: Most of the time, we don't think about why we do what we do. It is hidden deep in a belief system that we didn't even choose - it "came with the territory"... at birth and through our early upbringing! Based on how our parents and siblings related to us and what we believed we needed to do to survive and be loved, our primary strength developed - unconsciously.

Attitudes: As we became conscious of our surroundings, we also added a secondary style that shaped or "flavored" our mindset and attitudes. We figured out how to win -"I'll be tough", "I'll be charming", "I'll be patient", "and I'll be clever." Our behaviors are now made up of our "winning formula"- our ticket to success, and love. This secondary style definitely affects the way others experienced our primary style. If we are primarily "task-oriented, active", people like us or like to fight with us because we don't run off crying.

Those of us with a "people-oriented, active" secondary style learned we could get further down the road as a friendly, engaging, inspiring leader.

If we were "task oriented, active" as a primary style, but had developed our "task-oriented, passive secondary style, people would note that we could be much more focused on getting the job done, (but we weren't very warm and friendly!)

Actions: As life progresses, we keep choosing similar (successful) actions. These actions became our internal and external behaviors, which we practiced over and over again; it "seemed" that life was supposed to be lived this way. We didn't question or change it and nothing was "wrong" with it. It just got us to the end of the same roads... predictable (to someone outside watching us) ... but not to us. However, it did shape our style.

Results: When we repeated behaviors that worked (won), all was well. When we did the same behaviors and lost, we wondered, "Why do these things keep happening to me?" We seldom challenged them... But we can, as we better understand ourselves with DISC.

The Rubber Band Theory of Behavior

We are all a combination of the various styles (DISC) and operate within them all. Like a rubber band that stretches and flexes and changes its shape around different sized boxes, when the tension is let off, it comes back to a particular shape. That shape in humans is what we identify as their personality or behavioral style; it shows up on our profile in the DISC.

Our primary way of behaving with others works, and has been successful for us, so we do what we do because it makes us feel good... and because it works. It is our natural, "knee jerk", and instinctive way of behaving. We must be careful however, of the resulting "blind-spots."

Our Blind Spots are characteristics from our style that may not be making us happy or successful with others. It is in these times that we need to ask:

- WHY DO I DO WHAT I DO?
- Which characteristics am I using?
- Why is the other person reacting to me in a conflicted way?
- What did I do?
- How did they take that?
- What do I have to do to get what I want?

The good news is, once we understand style, these issues just seem to disappear!

We are not limited by or locked into our behavioral pattern. In DISC we assign each behavior to a letter, like a language. D, I, S, and C — as you look at your graphs; you'll see that you use some styles more than others. These are the ones that show up with a point in the upper half of the graph.

To follow are samples of graphs which will help you really see what everyone else already knows about you and how you behave. Understanding these graphs, and using them for dialog as a coach will move you ahead in helping your coachee become more aware of themselves and how to effectively interact with others, increasing their Emotional Intelligence.

"People who come from dysfunctional families are not destined for a dysfunctional life."

Bo Bennett

Chapter 6:
DISC Graphs and "D's"

How to Read the DISC Profile Graphs

If you have not done so yet, it is highly recommended that you stop your studies here and take the online DISC[7] profile for yourself (and you might do others as required if taking this course for credit). If you are already familiar with the DISC, then you can soldier on with this chapter to take a DISC profile, go to www.vision.edu/

A Typical Profile

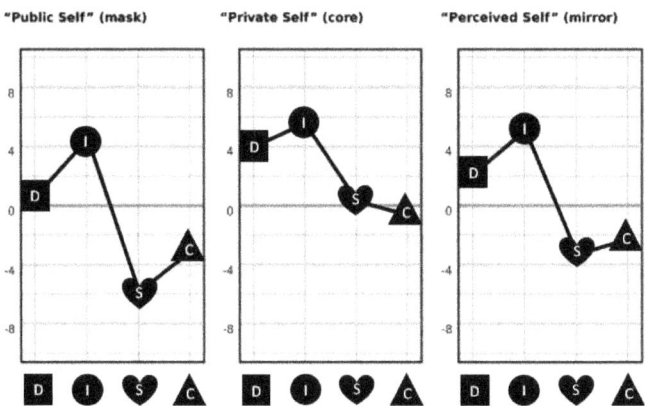

Find the letter that is your highest point on your Summary Graph. That would be either the D, the I, the S, or the C. You may have two that are equally high, or very close.

---

[7] Used by permission Copyright @2005 PeopleKeys

If you have no clear highest point on the Summary Graph, then use your Internal Graph as we describe in more detail these characteristics of D, I, S, and C.

The terms describing the letter that is your highest point should reflect the characteristics that you generally prefer to use as you relate to other people, in the setting you were focusing on when taking the profile (home, work, etc).

In coaching, a brief description, as provided here can help our coachee receive maximum benefit from the profile.

You can also use this information as you think of your friends or family members. Try to figure out what their highest point might be, and then you will begin to get the answers to "Why do we do what we do?"

Remember, people are a combination of these characteristics, and so a simple definition of your personality with only one characteristic will not be sufficient. Later in this book, we will describe various combinations of these characteristics. But for now, let's concentrate on the high point in your profile. That style is your Primary style and will incorporate most of the characteristics you tend to use more often than others. Other people know you by this style and, while your External style will change with the job or role you are doing, your Internal style will usually remain constant.

The primary style from your Internal Graph is what we like to say "leaks" out when you're not looking! It is your instinctive response to pressure and stress, and it is what most people experience of you. Let's take the D first...

ALL ABOUT D's (Remember, these are generalizations that are generally true)

Phil the Pill

For example, Phil is a high D...I mean really high, with little else to balance him out. As such, he is an aggressive, go for it, controlling person, at least at work. It is important to note however, at home, he does the dishes, helps with other chores, and frankly defers to his wife that he calls the Boss...though she is anything but bossy. Anyway, as we look at D's, keep in mind that the environment makes a difference...and probably who you are with.

Phil came for coaching after having been fired for being too controlling and aggressive at his last job. He was looking for help in developing a better style, and in also finding a career path with less stress (much of which he caused no doubt) and higher emotional rewards. As you will see from the study on Healthy vs Dysfunctional Families, Phil's was highly dysfunctional, and we have to deal with some of that, but overall he was healthy with enough insight to gain from coaching, and eventually found a new job with less stress.

D, again, stands for Dominance. D's like to control or dominate their environment. D's are often impatient with themselves, and with others. D's hate to wait around for us to talk about others.

Do you know a person with a very high D characteristic?

D's are usually fast-paced, task-oriented people. They thrive on the challenge of solving problems. D-styled people are quick decision-makers. They don't wait to be given authority; they take it. Don't bog these people down with fluff or details; the results are what interest them.

D's are most comfortable when they can control the environment. They work best when they are free from controls and supervision. The D group often runs roughshod over others. They overcome opposition to get the job done as they see life as basically an antagonistic environment.

Here's what we mean... When D's go on vacation they want to drive the entire 500 miles... in one day... without stopping of course, if possible. Can't you just hear the conversation in the family car? The 8-year-old daughter says, "Daddy I have to go to the bathroom!" The D daddy replies, "NO, you do not." Finally, the D relents, "OK, we will stop at the first Shell gas station that is next to McDonalds. Then you can go to the bathroom, we'll get gas and we can pick up our lunch at the same time. It shouldn't take us more than 7 or 8 minutes!"

Everything must be done quickly, or D's become bored. They lose interest and they are never satisfied. It takes change and challenge to keep their interest. Getting the job done is more important than the people who are doing the job.

D's dislike people who fail to perform up to their expectations. D's are good at summarizing, but communicating their expectations is not their gift. They don't listen very well, and tend to finish your sentences for you!

D's frequently make quick decisions, and they have an opinion on just about everything. They are outspoken, even when their opinion is not requested. D's can be quite blunt.

D's may be sharp in their criticism. They will never be accused of being too tactful. They don't like to watch others fail... and it is so tempting for them to say to you, "Get out of the way, kid. Let me show you how to do it"

D's have often been successful using these types of behavior to the degree that pushing other people around has worked for them; D's will try to control other people. For example, most D's don't explain how to do the job very well. "Just do it son!" with the unspoken threat... "And you better do it right!"

Some D's may be able to explain a task well, but only because, in the past, this has worked well for them. If quickness is of high enough value to the D, then breaking the job down into understandable parts may be worth it. D's may not be direct or blunt, if being subtle produces a higher or a quicker return.

D's weigh the reward-value of changing their instinctive behavior. They do what they do, because their success in using Dominance gives them competence. They generally have a very high ego strength. This ego strength sometimes comes across as unjustified self-confidence. Have you ever known a D who would admit to being lost? One who would stop and ask how to get somewhere? No, the D says, "I have a good sense of direction. We'll be there in a few minutes (This does not mean all men are "Ds")." Other people tolerate D's - not necessarily because D's are always right, but because they would rather let the D have their way than fight them! Guess which styles have the most trouble being with D's (if you are a high S or C or low I), you probably have personal experiences you could share... IF you wanted to share!

So, let's summarize:

- D's want freedom... from restrictions and authority.
- D's will tell you that rules are different for different people and that they know the "important" rules.
- D's never drive the speed limit — and they are proud of it! But try putting your car in a D's reserved parking space; now, THAT is breaking the rules!
- D's like change and a variety of activities and responsibilities are important to D's. They bore easily. Direct, brief responses to questions are all that are required by these D's. Long explanations either "show your weakness" or lose the attention of the D.
- They are "results oriented", as opposed to "people oriented"... Unless people are important to the results! Measurable performance is what counts on the D's scorecard!
- If deadlines are important, these need to be explained to the D —explained as a part of the "results expected." Thus...

In dealing with D's, be specific and direct.

- The D exerts control with the confidence that their decision will be a winner.
- Force of character provides control for the D.

- Details and accuracy are considered less significant than reaching conclusions.
- D's are ready to move on to the next challenge.

So, what will help a "D"? To balance your style on a team, you need others around you who:

- Weigh the pros and cons
- Calculate risks
- Use caution
- Structure a more predictable environment
- Research the facts
- Deliberate before deciding
- Recognize the needs of others

Further, a high "D" needs to:

- Learn to pace yourself better and know when and how to relax… especially with others. They want you around but may be afraid to reach out to you because of your past reactions.
- Start taking an interest in others and learn more about the needs of their style.
- Verbalize the reasons for your conclusions and your thinking (others like to feel included instead of just "told" and those people who are trying to "raise their D" will appreciate learning how a D thinks!)
- Let people know you are aware of existing sanctions or rules and why you are choosing to do something differently.
- Understand that everyone needs other people at times, including people like you!

- Accept the importance of existing limits and ways of doing things, even if you disagree.

So, if you have a High D in your life, this can help.

- Support their goals and objectives.
- Keep your relationship with them business-like and task-oriented.
- Recognize their ideas and accomplishments.
- Be precise, efficient and well organized.
- Provide alternative actions with brief supporting analysis.

Think you know enough about D's? (We always must remember to deal with the D's first. Otherwise, they get fidgety and we lose their attention! Now let's talk about the 'I's! (They love it when you do!)

To succeed in sales, simply talk to lots of people every day. And here's what's exciting – there are lots of people!

Jim Rohn

Chapter 7:
All About I

Samantha is an interior decorator that loves to talk. Whether planning a job or working it, she is the center of attention…and she loves to love! As a High I, she is very high energy at work, and in her case, equally high energy (some would say high maintenance) at home and other social settings. She just loves to be with people. Prison to her would be acceptable if she had multiple cellmates to talk with…but after a while, she might not live to tell about her friends in prison. Anyway, Samantha is somewhat typical of a High I…an influencer who is the life of the party and needs social interaction almost 24/7. She is a handful, but like all types, in the right environment and right situation, is invaluable to a team.

High I'S are called INFLUENCERS because they not only are fast-paced but they are the most outwardly People-Oriented of the styles. They love to talk and they are always inviting others to stop by and visit.

These are the ones you know as "People-people." They prefer to be around others and, while they can always enthrall an interviewer and get most any job, they would rather die than be shut up in an office all day or have to work by themselves for too long. They are the fun group, the huggers, and the party people. They are enthusiastic, entertaining, and love to help others. Popularity is important to the 'I's, who get their job done by making allies with others in a favorable environment.

Let me draw a distinction between an I and a D. Christmas brings out the major differences in people for example…

Opening Presents: Let's imagine a high D getting a Christmas present. What does a High D do as soon as a present is put in his hands? "Open" is too gentle of a word. He just RIPS it open!

Someone says, "Save the bow!" The D says, "What bow? Oh well, it was torn anyway."

He jerks the box open. Let's say it was a new PlayStation and it comes with a 42-page instruction book. Does a High D read the instruction book? Of course not! "Who needs instructions? I know how to operate this thing!" He plugs it in and blows it up. The high D won't demean himself by reading the instructions. It takes too long! It is a "waste of time" and, it postpones the need for instant gratification.

When the 'I' is opening Christmas presents, what is the first thing she does? Yes. She looks at the card to find out who sent it! "Oh, isn't that nice?" she says. Then she opens it carefully. Her first reaction? "A PlayStation!" "Gee, I didn't give John anything this nice. I don't want him to think I'm cheap!"

High I's are concerned about the opinions of other people, because they are confident that if they know other people, if they understand other people, if they help other people, then other people will help them. Let's put it this way... have you ever really disliked someone who liked you a lot?

If I say to you, "You are one of the sharpest people I've met in a long time"; well, right away, you would know that I'm either trying to sell you something, or that I'm one of the most perceptive observers of human beings that you've ever met!

Most people who like you, you'll like them too. And High I's discovered that a long time ago! They have a very positive attitude.

Here's the way they would describe their organization. "With the kind of people we have in our company, there's no telling what we could do." The key phrase is, "no telling." They believe anything is possible! But nothing specific needs to be documented!

High I's have big dreams. They set big goals. They have big ideas. High I's are dreamers. They are also spontaneous, or in yesterday's slang, they are "laid back." "Whatever you want to do is OK with me." "Want to have a party?" "Sure!" High I's are always ready - anytime, anywhere. Any excuse to be with other people…

(But the High D usually decides where to go! High I's don't care.)

Take lunch, for an example. A High I will take two hours for lunch. It doesn't matter what or where he's eating, it is just the conversation that's important, it's getting to know people, and it's the fun and pleasure of being around others.

The High D says: "30 minutes is much too long for lunch. It's a waste of time." The High I has no sense of time - around pleasant company. In fact, if you send three High I's out to lunch, they may NEVER come back!

High I's are very persuasive people. The word "charisma" was invented by a High I about another High I. They learned a long time ago that people love to buy, rather than being sold. They understand that if they can help me "buy" an idea, buy a product, or buy an association with another individual, then I will not only pay good money for it, but I'll probably pay more for it if I think it is MY idea.

In sales: A high D wants to go for a close immediately in a selling situation. The D doesn't often have the patience it takes to go through the romance that is involved in the selling process. The 'I' considers a good one-on-one relationship absolutely necessary to securing the order.

High D's and I's are both good sales people. But they take completely different approaches. High D's wants to go for the jugular. High 'I's forget to have the contract signed. The High I's will tell you that "it doesn't really matter; the other guy likes me so much, we don't even need a contract!"

High I's are good listeners - not necessarily attentive listeners, but they give off 'listening signals.' For example, High I's make friendly eye contact. I's are not as suspicious as D's. D's are so suspicious, even their eye contact is intense and probing.

High I's will look you right in the eye and sit forward in the chair and open their eyes big and bright, like they are hearing something for the first time - and you are pontificating on the most important information that they have ever encountered! You like talking to I's because they are so receptive to what you are saying. Now, they might not be hearing what you are saying, but they give off great listening signals.

Can you see the difference between an 'I' and a D listening to you? The friendly I vs. the bored D, drumming his fingers on the table, looking up at the ceiling, impatiently waiting for you to finish, so he can speak?

I's are very responsive to you. Even if their responses are vague, remember; they want to please you! The High I says, "We'll have to finish that job just as soon as we can, you know what I mean?" or "We've been working very hard to get what you need, but, you know, the weather's been bad" Or the Classic response... "Nooo Problem!" All vague generalities; High I's get away with it!

They get away with it because... you like them! High I's have lots of confidence because they have lots of friends!

Let's summarize the 'I's pattern: High I characteristics and why they do what they do...

- High I people - relationships are very important to their job satisfaction.
- The 'I' needs to have the opportunity to appreciate others, and to be appreciated.
- They have a tendency to be highly verbal, and physically active. Your high school quarterback and Homecoming Queen were likely High I's.
- They have an enjoyment of activities that provide for them freedom from detail. The I is excellent at getting the job started; not quite as good at following it up or its implementation.

- They seek opportunities to motivate people and to sell their ideas.

The High I would never perform well in a role that required isolation. (Can you imagine a High I bookkeeper?) They need people interaction.

- I's need assistance in translating their enthusiasm into actions and results, since "how to" is not as important as having other people to help the 'I' follow through.

- I's are able to control their environment through their personality and their friendship- we enjoy associating with High I's.

- They have a tendency to be excessively optimistic about results because High I's are dreamers.

- They can provide inspiration for others who have the responsibility of making things work… on a day by day basis.

- High I's have difficulty in activities requiring time management. They often need to be reminded that it is now time to "move on."

High I Tips for Being More Effective (your "blind spot' lies within this list.)

- Learn to develop more organized, systematic approaches to doing things - including following through with consistency in using these methods.

- Become more aware of others in ways that involve more realistic expectations and objective views of others.

- Understand how and when to be more firm and direct (in a non-judgmental manner) in dealing with less favorable situations.

- Accept the importance of completing works/agreements with people according to priority commitments and deadlines for them.

To balance your style on a team, you need others around you who:

- Concentrate on the task
- Seek facts
- Respect sincerity
- Develop systematic approaches
- Prefer dealing with things to dealing with people
- Take a logical approach
- Demonstrate individual follow through

Here are some tips for people in relationship with High I's

- Support their opinion, ideas and dreams
- Be entertaining and fast moving; don't hurry the discussion
- Try not to argue - you can seldom win
- Summarize in writing who is to do what, where, and when
- Use testimonials and incentives to positively affect decisions.

Conclusion

High "I's" can be an asset for a team as they provide positive energy for a productive community of co-workers. Most truly charismatic leaders have at least a good amount of I.

"It's the steady, quiet, plodding ones who win in the lifelong race."

Robert W. Service

Chapter 8: All About S

Ralph started his life as the middle child of 5 kids. He was not an outstanding athlete, nor a stellar student, but he was one thing for certain…he was a steady Eddie. As loyal as they come, you could always count on Ralph to show up and do his best. From High School he joined the Navy, worked his way up to a Chief, and retired to then join the local school district as a janitor, where he worked another 20 years, finally retiring. In church he was a deacon, at home a steady partner, as a father a good role model…you get it, he was steady as they come…not necessarily exciting, but without doubt, the best friend and most loyal worker you could ever want. That's Ralph.

High "S"

With that, let's move along to our S's who have been patiently waiting for us to finish!

All About "S"

We had to deal with those pushy D's and I's first because they are soooo impatient! They just could not wait to hear all about themselves!

Finally! We are getting down to what is important…the people who MAKE things happen instead of just talking about it… the S's and C's!!!

ALL ABOUT HIGH S's

Like the Influencers, this group is also people-oriented but at a much slower pace. The S group does not like to make quick decisions. They like to do things the way they always did. These are the "worker bees" in a company. The S behavioral style is patient and loyal. They also are excellent at listening to people and calming others when they get upset. S behavioral types get their best work done by co-operating with others.

When you find, and recognize one of these people - smile at them! They are the ones who do all the work! S's are the ones who hold our organizations together. Their controlled, deliberate pace creates the stability needed to keep the work flowing. They are the ones that keep things predictable... add stability to our lives. They know how it has to be done... how it has been done in the past, and they provide a sense of continuity for the organization.

S's are patient with others, and are the best at getting along with many different personalities. They can work well with all the other types. It takes patience to work well with D's, and S's don't get upset when the D's explode. They say inside, "It doesn't matter, he doesn't know what he's talking about anyway." Or, "He'll change his mind by tomorrow, so why argue... just let him find out for himself!"

S's "clean up" behind D's. D's make big pronouncements about all the things they are going to do, and S's get it done for them. S's don't worry about High I's either. In their opinion, they have learned that "the 'I' doesn't have any idea what he is talking about... he'll forget about his latest new idea within 24 hours anyway"! "It's OK."

The S knows that in the long run, it is the person who produces that receives the ultimate reward.

When the National Economy is in trouble, the management will look around and think: "maybe we need to cut some of this overhead." Then they start deciding what to cut. There are few patterns that we know of in business that determines what kinds of jobs get cut - sales jobs, purchasing jobs, secretarial jobs - sometimes all these jobs are vulnerable. There may be, however, a predictable pattern in terms of profile style patterns. The first people to go are some of those D's; you never did like them very well anyway! The second people to go are some of the 'I's. We never knew what they did, anyway.

The last people to go are the S's. The company could not function without the S's! They are the people who know how to do the job. They've got the system down pat. There is an S that runs the Accounting Systems, There's an S that is your hospital nurse. There's an S that runs the service department... they are invaluable! They know they are invaluable. They have high job security because they know they are special. They do their job well, and in detail.

S's are controlled. It is very difficult to judge how they are reacting, unless you ask specific questions. But S's are not aware that you don't know how they feel. They frequently feel that "you should know", even if you haven't been told. S's are sensitive and loyal people. They are concerned with how the jobs are going to be done. The D's only concern what's going to be accomplished; is the bottom line. The 'I's are concerned about "who is going to do it with me?"

Techniques are important to the S. S's are generally good under pressure, - if they can focus on HOW to do what needs to be done. Their deliberateness and their emotional control will help them to accomplish those results.

A summary of some of the S characteristics:

- S's are quite predictable and prefer using established procedures
- S's will perform well with consistent conditions.
- They need specialization in areas where routine can be controlled.
- S's are concerned more with process than with the end result.
- The High S knows HOW to do the job and is persistent in their actions, once their goals have been established.
- An S will never be accused of being lazy.

They will be able to function well when they are under pressure if they are familiar with what is required, how the job is to be done, and can follow their established routines. And if they receive all that, then long and constant pressure will not hamper their performance.

- They need reasons for change.
- They need time for evaluation of the new direction.
- They need to be involved in the planning for change.

The S will not accept new ideas without personal involvement and an understanding of the need for a new direction. Further, an S requires a definition of their role and function in the new procedure; a description of their involvement in how they can contribute to positive results.

An S needs opportunity for feedback. They will not state their opinion, unless they are asked.

They need encouragement to expand their skills into new areas.

For an S to develop and grow, they need to be challenged, and encouraged, by those around them. Their strength is on handling assignments requiring follow through and adherence to procedures.

Back to Opening Presents:

It appears to others that S's get more presents than the D's and 'I's because the stack is larger around their chair. It is not that they get more presents; it is that it takes them longer to open their gifts.

The D will say, "We need to keep a record of these gifts." The 'I' chimes in and continues... "Yes... so we will know what to give them next year!" Who ends up with this job? The S of course, Why? There is already a small gray metal file box next to their chair that the S uses to record each gift. The cards are alphabetically filed with a list of the gifts received for the past five years - for the whole family - and cross-referenced with their Christmas card list! A High S can tell you what Aunt Suzy gave him for Christmas five years ago. A High D couldn't even tell one gift they received last year! The High I's have it all confused. They say, let's see, was it the CD that Janice gave me? Or was it the book? Oh, it doesn't matter -she's such a sweet girl.'

Some high S's may not have the card file, but they have a superior memory. They pay attention to the process even when it is just opening the gifts. They deliberately pace their actions and show concern for the people that are involved in the process... the Aunt Sally's of the world.

High S TIPS FOR BEING MORE EFFECTIVE (your 'blind spot" lies within this list.)

- Learn how to better handle the reality of unexpected and ongoing change.
- Become more aware of when to appropriately delegate to other people to achieve desired results.
- An S must understand how to be more assertive with people in taking charge of certain situations, accepting the opportunity to grow by learning to do new and different things, including a variety of ways other than your own standard approach.

To balance your style on a team, you need others around you who:

- React quickly to unexpected change
- Stretch toward the challenges of an accepted task
- Become involved in more than one thing
- Are self-promoting
- Apply pressure on others
- Work comfortably in an unpredictable environment
- Delegate to others
- Are flexible in work procedures

- Can contribute to the work

Some tips for people in relationship with High S's

- Support their feelings by showing personal interest and actively listening
- Move along in an informal, slow manner
- Allow them time to trust you
- When you disagree, discuss personal feelings
- Provide guarantees and personal assurances

Conclusion

If you are coaching a high S, your initial goal is to gain trust through active listening and affirming their steadiness. Most will want to move forward in making changes, but not at a rapid pace but slow and steady indeed. Every organization needs men and women who are consistent, and who will hang in no matter the problem. They are worth their weight in gold.

Chapter 9: All About C

Willamina was born in the South, the last child of 4, and loved to order her life from as far back as anyone can remember. She was not obsessive-compulsive, but simply loved making things look right. There was a right way or a wrong way, and Willamina was always wanting to the do the right thing, and expected others to do likewise.

When she grew up, she recognized the gift that was her organizational skills, becoming a bookkeeper, eventually an accountant. However, she wanted to move beyond just doing numbers and wanted help to move into management, maybe even ownership of her own business. That was why she was seeking help from a Coach.

The "C"

So on to the C's- who have been busy while they have been writing, editing and re-writing the procedures manual just one more time...

ALL ABOUT C'S

Our last group of behaviors falls into the C Section - Compliance to Rules and Regulation - A search for Competence: A desire for Accuracy.

C's are the slower paced, cautious, task-oriented people. They focus on the tiniest, most minute details in a project. They are concerned about doing the job right and will pay inordinate amounts of attention making sure it is. Unless quality will be improved, the C does not like sudden or abrupt changes. They get their job done by working with the existing circumstances to promote quality.

C's may postpone actions and decisions until they are sure they can get it absolutely right.

C's are concerned with the correct process... the best path towards the goal - with a premier product or superior result.

C's are the Critics of the world — but critic doesn't mean negative - it can be either. A critic provides a review - an observation.

The High C's of the world stand back about three paces and take it all in. They are observers of human behavior. They are judges of other people.

At Christmas time, they open their PlayStation... here is what goes through their mind...

> "Let's see, this is last year's model. The newer model would have been better. I wonder if they got that on sale, or paid full price... I would have waited for a sale of course... and on they go.

C's collect trivia - Where they store it, I don't know. You ask a C who is a sports buff, extraneous questions like... "There was a player named Gil Cohen who played for the Washington Senators in the early 50's.

"What was his lifetime batting average?" They can tell you!

Don't get into arguments with High C's... They always win! They remember the smallest of details.

If you challenge a C on how he is doing his job, the C will say," If you look at specification 3622, it's on page 42 in the third column. You'll find the test data we are supposed to be using is from ASTM 31." And they are right! These are information-oriented people.

One must be careful when working with or trying to spot a high C. You might assume fastidiousness and a strict regimentation. Many C's are sloppy... but they know where everything is! Take a look at their desk! It is loaded with papers and file folders, invoices. It is a complete mess. You might think, this can't be a high C, but they will know something about every piece of paper on that desk. They might not be organized for you and me to see, but they are organized mentally.

Their mission is to be correct - to be right. High C's are good people to have in quality control. The only problem is their desire for quality is far too superior for the quality necessary in some situations. Sometimes High C's can set standards that are very costly to the company and are not really called for in established procedures.

High C's may be loners. They are more reserved than D's and I's. High C's can sometimes sound like D's because they can occasionally scream as loud as a D and sometimes be as obnoxious as D's. The difference is, the D wants it done HIS way... the C wants it done... the RIGHT way. And the C is almost always right... once their decision has been made.

C's can therefore cloak themselves in self-righteousness. High C's can PROVE they are right!

High C's have a common question... "Why?"

Why did you do it that way? Why didn't you do it this way? Why aren't we committing ourselves to this contract? Why didn't we wait? Why didn't we bring in John? Why, Why, Why, Why. Why?"

C's also have a lot of confidence. It is confidence in the correctness of their answer.

Let's look at what the C's need to get the most out of them (what they are concerned with the most.)

WHAT C's NEED:

- C's like detailed explanations and descriptions of their assignments. Remember, they want to know the reasons for everything.
- They like a specific approach to decision making and they always want to know, "Exactly HOW do I do what I do?"

- C's need procedures and sequences to help them determine the end result.

The process will always be challenged by the high C; not just the dream or the bottom line, but HOW we will accomplish the projected results.

Analysis is used by the C as a control for unnecessary change. C's are slow. They want to look in depth to see if change is really needed. They use planning and questioning as instruments for control.

- They tend to think by discovery
- They ask open-ended questions.
- The C will always question directives. They will not accept orders or suggestions until they know WHY a decision is to be made.
- They take a long time to look; to analyze if a decision is required.

Personal decisions are guided by a need to be RIGHT. Therefore, testing is needed for all potential solutions.

Bring to a C the REASONS for your suggested change. The C must have the facts to support the ideas. Involvement in planning for change strengthens the commitment from C's. They want to be able to view all the people, all the facts and all of the opinions before making their commitments.

High C TIPS FOR BEING MORE EFFECTIVE (your "blind spot" lies within this list.)

- Learn to develop a greater tolerance for conflict and human imperfection, including realistic approaches to productively prevent and minimize both.
- Become more aware of the importance of directly communicating and discussing your views with others about matters of benefit to either or both.

- Understand the different types of talents and interest levels of individuals and their usefulness in achieving desired objectives.
- Accept with a greater sense of true self-esteem the importance of what you are, as a worthwhile person in your own right, rather than only for what you do.

To balance your style on a team, you need others around you who:

- Desire to expand themselves
- Delegate important tasks
- Make quick decisions
- Use policies only as guidelines
- Compromise with the opposition
- State unpopular positions

Key tips for being in relationship with C's

- Support their organized, thoughtful approach
- Demonstrate through actions, not words
- Be systematic, exact, organized, and prepared
- List advantages and obvious disadvantages of any plan
- Provide guarantees and proof that actions can't backfire.
- Refer to these lists often. They will prevent lots of misunderstandings between you and others.

Conclusion

All high behavioral styles have their challenges. No style is better than another, just different, and learning about different styles, and your own, can be fascinating, informative, and effective in building teams and relationships in general. Conclusion, now that you are getting the hang of it, let's look further at your profile.

"When you are behaving as if you loved someone, you will presently come to love him. If you injure someone you dislike, you will find yourself disliking him more. If you do him a good turn, you will find yourself disliking him less."

C.S. Lewis, *Mere Christianity*

Chapter 10: Read On

How to Read the Graphs

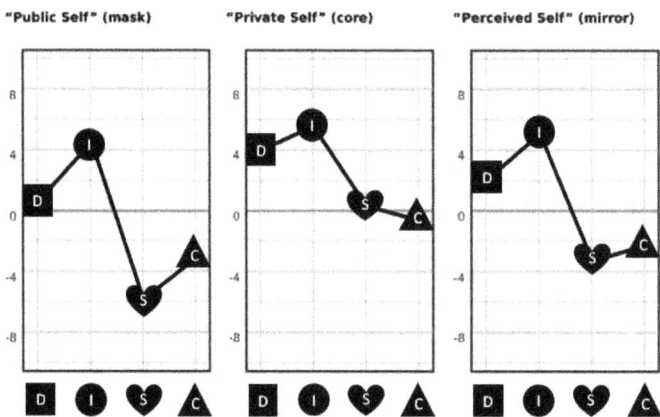

Now that we better understand the High D's, I's, S's and C's, let's look at the graphs in a typical DISC report to see what they tell us.

Internal Graph

Your internal graph describes YOU UNDER PRESSURE. It shows up when you get backed into a corner — when there is only a half-hour to do the job and you don't have all the information... or when the inspector is going to be there in 30 minutes. Or when the bank calls and says they want to see you right away - or when one of your best people tells you they are getting ready to resign.

The External Graph is our mask. This is the behavior that on a daily basis people identify with the "real you."

The Summary Graph is your self-perception... this is a combination of your mask and your instinctive reaction to pressure. We can change between these three graphs. As an example, perhaps your D is fairly high in the Adapted Graph - the way you see yourself at work. It indicates that your job requires a lot of decision making, yet in the Internal Graph, under pressure, you tend to always let stronger people take charge... which is shown by your D going down.

Another example. Suppose we have a D below the midline that jumps up under pressure. This would indicate an explosive and temperamental person who responds negatively to pressure. Perhaps this person has found that losing their temper gets results. We do what we do because it has proven effective for us in getting the results we want.

Perhaps your I is fairly high in your External (Adapted) Graph. Normally you are a talker, but under pressure (Internal Graph), you're talking (I) goes down and you're doing (S) goes up. Perhaps you don't normally like routine assignments, but, under pressure, your ability to focus your attention rises.

Let's look at other examples of changing styles under pressure.

If your C is below the centerline in the External Graph, and it goes to the top in the Internal Graph, this would mean that you don't think you are expected to concentrate on following specific procedures. But it also means that, under pressure, you would tend to slow down and concentrate on accuracy. In other words, it would take PRESSURE to get you to comply with the rules.

Pressure can take many forms; it might mean deadlines, a desire to win, or close inspection.

Another interesting comparison can be made between the External Graph, Adapted Graph and the Summary Graph; it displays how comfortable we are in our current role. Here, we are comparing what we think others expect us to be with what we think we really are. In other words, if you are High I in your External Graph, and a very Low I in the Summary Graph, you may be experiencing some discomfort because you need to try to communicate more and this is difficult for you. You might be expected to be friendly with people, when your normal reaction would be withdrawal and isolation.

If your D is high in the Adapted Graph and low in the Summary Graph, you may be experiencing pressure to be more dominant and to exercise more control and authority.

If your S is high in the Adapted Graph and low in the Summary Graph, you may need to concentrate more and follow through. You may not feel comfortable with this level of activity and this sameness of repetitive tasks. You may want more change in your life than you currently find.

Look at your graphs again. Think about what changes, if any, that pressure makes in your behavior. Do you agree with the words and patterns that describe you? Do you want to continue to act in the ways described in these profiles? Do you want to try to use more or less of the D, or the I, or the S, or the C?

Remember that there is no RIGHT way for your graphs to look. No correct profile. They are only a reflection of you and the way you react under different circumstances.

It is also important to remember that this profile can look significantly different when it measures your behavioral style in different environments. There is perhaps a difference in your work behavioral style and your style at home - the way you act with close friends and the way you act with new people.

WYSIWYG - (WHAT YOU SEE IS WHAT YOU GET)

Some people are the same in all three Graphs and in all environments. They are the same in all situations. They don't ever change how they do what they do. This can be both positive and negative because sometimes CHANGE in our behavior can help us cope. If we are D's, perhaps we need to use more S or C. It is true that if we don't change from our Adapted Graph to the Internal

Graph, we are more PREDICTABLE - our behavior is very stable under pressure. Others know what to expect from us, even in difficult circumstances.

Does my profile indicate my intelligence? NO! You can be a smart D or a dumb D. A smart I or a dumb I. A smart S or a dumb S. A smart C or a dumb C. These profiles don't measure intelligence; neither do they measure experience, or technical capabilities. Rather, the DISC tells us how we use our abilities, and how we communicate in relationships.

HOW TO READ THE STYLE CARD

One of the most useful applications of the Style Card technique is in describing a personality's motivators and, correspondingly, their de-motivators. This can help coaches to adapt their style and approach to a particular individual. In a more specific sense, this information can also be useful in motivating an individual to choose a particular course of action.

A name has been given for each of the four main types – Driver (D), Communicator (I), Planner (S) and Analyst (C). Each of these has an associated set of motivators and de-motivators.

Driver: Achievement and control motivate Drivers. It is very important to them to feel that they are driving a situation (hence the name of the style) and they will consequently be more receptive if they feel in full control of a situation. Should they feel unduly pressured, they will be less likely to accept an idea and they react particularly badly to direct orders, whatever their source.

Communicator: As you might expect from the name of this style, positive communication is the main motivator for this type of person. They wish to develop a real rapport with a person before reacting to specific ideas or proposals. Rejection is a factor that they find difficult to accept, and if they do not feel completely comfortable with someone (a rare situation for a confident person of this type) they will be far less likely to respond positively.

Planner: Time is the main motivator of the Planning style. They dislike sudden change or interruption, and need time and patience to adapt to new situations. If they are forced into a position they will react negatively; a more productive approach is to allow them to accommodate themselves to a suggestion in their own timescale. Their primary fear is radical or rapid change and not being included.

Analyst: Facts and details are the factors that analysts seek out. They need to be able to understand the implications and probable effects of a proposal before they can come to accept it, and this means a precise and methodical approach. Being forced to act without fully understanding a situation is a profound de-motivator for personalities of this type.

Each of the four intermediate types, as you might expect, combine the motivating factors of the two main styles between which they lie.

Assertive: Lying between the Driver and the Communicator, this type emphasizes and extends the Driver's desire for control into the field of social relations. Not only will the Assertive individual wish to build a strong relationship in order to feel motivated but they will also wish to feel that they hold a distinctly dominant position within that relationship.

Open: Open styles combine elements from the Communicator and the Planner. This means they will wish to take a patient, measured view of a situation but they will also wish to maintain positive relations with others. This can lead to some potential problems as the Open individual tries to balance their own need for calm, long-term appraisal with other people's demands for action.

Passive: Passive personality styles, incorporating elements of both the patient Planner and the factual Analyst, are especially reluctant to act without being entirely certain of their position, They need to feel that they are in command of all the facts, and that they can see all possible problems before they can accept an idea or adapt effectively to a new situation.

Controlled: Lying midway between the Driver and the Analyst, the Controlled type assumes an attitude of control, and will respond negatively to any perceived attempt of control or attempt to undermine this position. Unlike the pure Driver, however, they will tend to adopt a formal, structured approach, attempting to enforce their desires through rules and authority, rather than pure force of personality.

HOW TO GET OTHERS TO DO WHAT YOU WANT THEM TO DO?

Try the new awareness out by observing people you come into contact with each day. Use some of the following communications tips as practice for meeting their needs:

Checklist for Communicating

When communicating with a person who is ambitious, forceful, decisive, strong-willed, independent, and goal oriented (A High D who Dominates Problems)

Do	Don't
Be clear, specific, brief and to the point	Talk about things that are not relevant to the issue.
Stick to business	Leave loopholes or cloudy issues
Come prepared with support material in a well-organized "package"	Appear disorganized

A person who is magnetic, enthusiastic, friendly, demonstrative and political (A High I who influences People)

Do	Don't
Provide a warm and friendly environment	Be cold, curt, or tight-lipped
Don't deal with a lot of details, (put them in writing).	Control the conversation
Ask "feeling" questions to draw their opinions or comments	Drive on with facts and figures, alternatives, abstractions

A person who is patient, predictable, reliable, steady, relaxed and modest (High S steadies the pace)

Do	Don't
Begin with a personal comment to break the ice	Rush headlong into business
Present your case softly and non-threateningly	Be domineering or demanding
Ask "How" questions to draw their opinions	Force them to respond quickly to your objectives.

A person who is dependent, neat, conservative, a perfectionist, careful, and compliant (High C- Complies to Procedures and Rules)

Do	Don't
Prepare your "case" in advance	Be giddy, casual, informal, loud
Stick to business	Push too hard or be unrealistic with deadlines
Be accurate and realistic	Be disorganized or messy

CAN I EVER CHANGE?

You can change who you have developed yourself to be... if you want to. People usually change only when they see a problem with what they are doing and acknowledge it to be causing a problem. Remember; you spent many years developing the "muscles" of what works about your style. It may take a long time to strengthen other characteristics you would prefer.

How do I change my behavior?

First, it is important to remember that Marston, the behavioral scientist who first named the four behavioral styles D, I, S, and C said:

"All people exhibit all four behavioral factors in varying degrees of intensity." - W.M. Marston, The Emotions of Normal People, 1928

Once you begin to recognize styles and notice which styles you are more comfortable being, you can also recognize the styles you are not like. Learn how you are different from the other styles and how to adapt your own style to meet their needs.

TIPS FOR CHANGING BEHAVIOR
- Take a step-by-step approach.
- Find a coach who is each of the styles you are not. *
- Go out for an evening or weekend to a place where lots of other people are and observe how they act.
- Practice your people-reading skills together.
- Strategize on ways to approach the different styles.
- Practice different approaches with people.
- Find out what works and what does not.
- Ask other friends for feedback on how you are doing.

Conclusion

One of the benefits of DISC is you don't need to remember all of this information, for, a good profile will provided excellent summaries for you, highly usable and almost magic for the client. Of course, a good coach will work to mirror each style to help their coachee understand these styles and modify theirs for greater effectiveness.

"I have always said that everyone is in sales. Maybe you don't hold the title of salesperson, but if the business you are in requires you to deal with people, you, my friend, are in sales."

Zig Ziglar

"The secret of man's success resides in his insight into the moods of people, and his tact in dealing with them."

J. G. Holland

Chapter 12:
Selling in Style with DISC

(Which is helpful in establishing a coaching practice!)

Notice what happens when you identify a person's style, and then customize the following phrases for use in your own sales presentation. A good coach will work to mirror each style to help their coachee understand these styles and modify theirs for greater effectiveness.

Sample Phrases to Sell to a High "D"

- This is new; there is nothing to compare to this product/service.

- Within just 24 hours you can have your own personalized behavioral style report on anyone in your team or company - anywhere in the world.

- This will provide you an opportunity to get credit for what you do. It is something you can call your own.

- This product can help you make decisions by providing accurate, up-to-the-minute information.

- We present your data in a quick, easy-to-read format.

Sample Phrases to Sell to a High "I"

- In making many business contacts, it is rare that I find individuals as enthusiastic and motivated as you!

- I was quite favorably impressed with the energy you share with others in your working environment.

- By combining our products/services with what you are presently doing, you will be even more successful in communicating with your employees.

- Others have gained professional recognition in adapting this product/service, and with your contacts, energy and enthusiasm, you can surpass even their achievements.

Sample Phrases to Sell to a High "S"

- We are a steady, reliable organization providing products and services for over 20 years.
- Our products and services will help you work smarter in 2017 and 2018 by helping you concentrate on your most valuable resources - your employees.
- We can help continue to keep your productivity high.
- Our product/service gives you security by helping to focus on communications with employees.

Sample Phrases to Sell to a High "C"

- Choosing our products/service is a wise decision that will stand up to your high standards of operation.
- This product/service provides accurate reports to assist you with managing and communicating with your employees.
- This product/service will make your work environment more secure without abrupt changes in operating procedure.
- Please review in detail the enclosed information and draw your own conclusions.
- With our product/service this is important. Let's set up several sessions where we can clarify all the possible alternatives.

RECRUITING IN STYLE

When you understand that a person's style is you can also tell what motivates each style - their GOALS (when positively motivated or energized) and their FEAR (when negatively energized) in a given situation - you can present your organization/ministry in terms that will motivate a potential recruit and utilize the profile in recruiting a potential client.

Disc Style	They WANT	They AVOID	They JOIN based on...	Your STRATEGY for recruiting them	Benefits of JOINING YOUR team
D	Results, Control	Losing control of environment; being taken advantage of	What your organization does for them	The potential impact of joining your organization	Results
I	People involvement, recognition	Rejection; loss of approval	Who is in your organization (and what they say about it)	Your organization's "appeal to people"	Recognition and enhanced relationship
S	Security, Stability	Sudden changes; Losing security	How your organization will help stabilize conditions for them	The support provided by your organization	Strong and Stable
C	Accuracy/ order	Criticism of performance; lack of standards	Why your organization is a logical investment for them	The "track record" of your organization	Concise, clear and accurate

Use the following charts to customize your sales strategies as you recognize yourself and your customer.

DISC Behavioral Recognition and Selling Strategies for the... D

Dominance/Driver/Choleric	Strength: Solving Problems Overuse: Impatient Emotion: Anger/Short fuse
Step 1: Know Yourself As a D Salesperson, you: Are Results (task) Oriented Want to close fast Tend to be Argumentative May try overpowering the person Like to win May not follow up properly May be unprepared Can handle several customers at once	Step 2: "Read" the person you're selling to and observe their EMOTION Extroverted Direct? = D (Emotion is ANGER) Friendly? = I (Emotion is OPTIMISM) Introverted and... Co-operative? = S (NON-EMOTIONAL) Analytical? = C (FEAR to break rules)
Step 3: when selling to...	Behavioral Style Match (BSM)... (1 great- 4 Poor)
D's (BSM= 2 Good) Looks for direct answers Likes: New products Notices: Green Walks: fast	I's (BSM= 2 Good) Looks for the Experience Likes: Showy products Notices: Red Walks: fast

Selling Strategy: Be direct Give alternatives Make sure you let them win (you too) They may disagree with facts They enjoy the "combat" (good match) Don't try to build a friendship Don't dictate to them Move quickly; they decide fast Do not try to overpower them	Selling Strategy: Be personal, friendly Slow down, take time Joke around and have fun Allow them to talk Provide recognition Don't talk down to them Talk about people Follow up often
C's (BSM= 4 Poor) Looks for information Likes: Proven products Notices: Yellow Walks: Straight Line	S's (BSM= 3 Fair) Looks for Security Likes: Traditional products Notices: Green Walks: Steady Pace
Selling Strategy: Give them the data Do not touch Be patient, slow Use flyers with data Give more information than you'd like Keep control	Selling Strategy: Slow down presentation Build trust Keep a People or Family Focus Give them the facts they need Make a logical presentation Get "little" agreements Listen carefully

Do not talk personally	Show sincerity in presentation
Do not be pushy	Don't control or dominate
	Do not close fast

DISC Behavioral Recognition and Selling Strategies for the… I

Influencing/Expressive/ Sanguine	Strength: Relating to people Overuse: Disorganized Emotion: Optimism
Step 1: Know Yourself: As an I Salesperson, you… Are Active (People) Oriented Are socially motivated so may over talk Are enthusiastic May over-promise due to optimism Tend to lack attention to details May close too slowly — or not at all	Step 2: "Read" the person you're selling to and observe their EMOTION Extroverted Direct? = D (Emotion is ANGER) Friendly? = I (Emotion is OPTIMISM) Introverted and… Co-operative? = S (NON-EMOTIONAL) Analytical? = C (FEAR to break rules)
Step 3: when selling to…	Behavioral Style Match (BSM)…(1 great- 4 Poor)
D's (BSM= 2 Good) Looks for direct answers	I's (BSM= 2 Good) Looks for the Experience

Likes: New products Notices: Green Walks: fast	Likes: Showy products Notices: Red Walks: fast
Selling Strategy: Be direct — do not touch! Give alternatives and stay business like Let them win (but you win too) Do not over promise Do not joke Confidently close, not over-power them	Selling Strategy: Have fun Don't waste time talking. Joke around Allow them to talk more than you.
C's (BSM= 4 Poor) Looks for information Likes: Proven products Notices: Yellow Walks: Straight Line	S's (BSM= 3 Fair) Looks for Security Likes: Traditional products Notices: Green Walks: Steady Pace
Selling Strategy: Keep your distance Do not touch Give them the facts, figures and proof Do not waste time Do not be personal Be friendly and direct Answer all their questions,	Selling Strategy: Give them the facts Slow down Be friendly, personal and earn their trust. Provide assurances of your promises Get "little" agreements Let them talk; Listen carefully; ask questions

| Be concerned with details | Follow up after the sale |

DISC Behavioral Recognition and Selling Strategies for the... S

Steadiness/Amiable/Phlegmatic	Strength: Co-operation Overuse: Possessiveness Emotion: Non-Demonstrative
Step 1: Know Yourself: As an S Salesperson, you... Are Passive — People Oriented Are a natural and personable salesperson Are steady and dependable Easily discouraged, low confidence Great on follow-through (May over-service) May give away money under pressure More enthusiasm; less facts May wait too long to close	Step 2: "Read" the person you're selling to and observe their EMOTION Extroverted Direct? = D (Emotion is ANGER) Friendly? = I (Emotion is OPTIMISM) Introverted and... Co-operative? = S (NON-EMOTIONAL) Analytical? = C (FEAR to break rules)
Step 3: when selling to...	Behavioral Style Match (BSM)... (1 great- 4 Poor)

D's (BSM= 2 Good) Looks for direct answers Likes: New products Notices: Green Walks: fast	I's (BSM= 2 Good) Looks for the Experience Likes: Showy products Notices: Red Walks: fast
Selling Strategy: Be confident; don't be intimidated Close sooner than normal Disagree with the facts - not the person. Do not be overpowered by them Let them win (you win too) They decide fast, so move faster, come on as strong as the "D" but be friendly	Selling Strategy: Allow them to talk, but keep focus Give minimal product knowledge Provide follow-up Give recognition to things they do or have done Listen to their stories Have fun with them "Jump" to close when ready
C's (BSM= 4 Poor) Looks for information Likes: Proven products Notices: Yellow Walks: Straight Line	S's (BSM= 3 Fair) Looks for Security Likes: Traditional products Notices: Green Walks: Steady Pace

Selling Strategy: Answer questions with facts Do not be too personal Be direct and friendly Do not touch Give them their space Do not fear their skeptical nature Follow through on details Give information, then close	Selling Strategy: Give them the facts Provide the assurances they need Be yourself Close when you feel you have their trust Assure them of the right decision Introduce them to managers, service managers, etc. Follow up after the sale

DISC Behavioral Recognition and Selling Strategies for the... C

Compliance/Analytical/ Melancholic	Strength: Careful Details, Quality Control Overuse: Critical Emotion Emotion: Fear (of breaking rules)
Step 1: Know Yourself: As a C Salesperson, you Are Passive - Task-Oriented Know product data May over-evaluate and over-use data Need more enthusiasm May have trouble selling products below your own standards Are well organized Are a good service provider	Step 2: "Read" the person you're selling to and observe their EMOTION Extroverted Direct? = D (Emotion is ANGER) Friendly? = I (Emotion is OPTIMISM) Introverted and... Co-operative? = S (NON-EMOTIONAL) Analytical? = C (FEAR to break

Tend toward "analysis"	rules)
Step 3: when selling to…	Behavioral Style Match (BSM)… (1 great- 4 Poor)
D's (BSM= 2 Good) Looks for direct answers Likes: New products Notices: Green Walks: fast	I's (BSM= 2 Good) Looks for the Experience Likes: Showy products Notices: Red Walks: fast
Selling Strategy: Touch high points of facts and figures Do not "over-data" Be brief, to the point Satisfy their strong ego Allow them to "win" (you win too!) Move quickly; they decide fast	Selling Strategy: Have a personal and friendly focus Listen to them as they talk Ask questions Don't talk down to them Show excitement about products Close earlier than normal
C's (BSM= 4 Poor) Looks for information Likes: Proven products Notices: Yellow Walks: Straight Line	S's (BSM= 3 Fair) Looks for Security Likes: Traditional products Notices: Green Walks: Steady Pace

Selling Strategy:	Selling Strategy:
Give them the data	Move slowly
Remain in control	Provide facts arid figures
Examine positives and negatives	Do not over-control or be too pushy.
Close earlier than you would expect	Provide assurances
Provide evidence	Develop trust
	Focus on reliability and service
	Personal talk allowed

Style Modification Strategies ("Shape Shifting")

The keys for maximizing your effectiveness in everyday situations and bringing out the best in others are:

Know your own style well and understand how you come across to others.

Be sensitive to the needs of those around you and adapt and blend your behavior according to those needs by adopting the following strategies.

Strategy: Decrease Assertiveness

- If you are a High D or High I: Ask more and tell less!
- Ask for opinions of others.
- Negotiate decision-making.
- Listen without interrupting.
- Adapt to the time needs of others.
- Allow others to assume leadership more often.

Strategy: Increase Responsiveness If you are a High C or High D: Control feelings less, show feelings more! Reveal feelings Pay personal compliments Be willing to spend time on the relationship. Engage in small talk – socialize. Be friendlier in language and behavior.	High D's Need to know: what it does/ When/ Cost Support their: Goals Save them: Time High I's Need to know: How it enhances status/ visibility Support their: Ideas Save them: Effort High C's Need to Know: How they can justify it logically Support their: Procedures Save them: Face High S's Need to know: how it will affect them personally Support their: Feelings Save them: Conflict

If you are a High C or High S: Tell more and ask less!

- Get to the point.
- Volunteer information.
- Be willing to disagree.
- Act on your convictions.
- Initiate conversation more.
- Strategy: Increase Assertiveness

Conclusion

As a part of our coaches' certification program, we require the student to complete the course on Behavioral Analysis developed by People Keys and Dr. Sandy Kulkin, its founder and graduate of our university. Further, you will be required to take and give several DISC profiles (one of many you will no doubt learn to use in your future practice), to become familiar with this powerful tool. It takes practice to get good at any profession, as it will with coaching, but with the power of DISC you will be way ahead of the game, and able to understand and communicate with the *head* of your client with accuracy and precision.

"Some strive to make themselves great. Others help others see and find their own greatness. It's the latter who really enrich the world we live in"

Rasheed Ogunlaru

Chapter 13:
The Process of Mentor/Coaching

Introduction

To enjoy a full and rich Coach/Mentor experience, regardless of the field, one needs both academic preparation and practical experience. Most assuredly, practical experience, supervision and mentorship are needed for every area of business; for working professionals and for life.

Unfortunately, many educational institutions have allowed to fall fallow this important component of learning: discipleship or mentorship leading to practical application of theory obtained in the classroom or other modality of learning.

The purposes of an education in the modern world are multiple. Whether one takes the purest view of the expansion of the mind, or the realist desire for significant employment, both are meaningful goals for student and instructor alike. In other words, knowledge and understanding must somehow translate into wisdom, or a practical outworking in the real world. It is the work of a mentor, where supervision by a qualified coach with a prepared student occurs, so that the working out of knowledge and understanding in a chosen field is realized. Thus, the purpose of this book is to assist the key individuals in this practical aspect of education/training to effectively function towards the common goal of the student in the real world.

Consequently, if you are a coach/mentor assigned to a student, you will want to assist your student in the developing of experience in practical and negotiated areas. Much experience can be gained within a local setting; however, depending on the needs of the assigned student, external experiences may be the order of the day. In either case, this mentor/coaching should have a focus on ensuring that the student has a well-rounded coaching experience.

In the ministry of Jesus, he combined teaching with doing, faith with action. It takes both to be successful in life and ministry. We all must learn to do our work with excellence. The operative word is "do".

Words of the Wise for the Coachee

For most students, working has been the goal of study, and the most anxiety producing aspect of your educational program. For one already working, doing so with greater skill and joy would be a realistic goal. One of the most frequently asked questions of a student (by parents and peers, let alone by self) is, "can I get a job with this certificate, diploma or degree, or a better one, more fulfilling"? The proper answer to this question is, "it depends". There are multiple factors affecting a person's ability to succeed in life, including job availability, flexibility/skill of the job candidate, perhaps the luck of the Irish! However, the future need not be filled with unnecessary anxiety.

We have hope in God… If indeed you are called to serve, he who has called you will assist you in making a way when there is no way. A solid coach can enhance your process.

We have a sound mind, in that, we have the ability to know if we "fit" in an area of service after having tried. No experience is without some redeeming value in itself, and of itself.

A healthy mentor/coach will enter into relationship with the student with a focus on helping the later to fully determine their direction for life, and develop a plan to achieve it… or at least get on the path in the right direction.

The Historic Precedent

Throughout history, mentor/teacher/ or student/disciple relationships have had significant importance. A brief review with comments will give a clear perspective, both positive and negative.

Ancient Times

Though the process for mentorship is not outlined in the ancient life, in Genesis, the transference of patterns, both positive and negative, can be seen in the lives of Abraham, Isaac, Jacob and Joseph. Through relationship, storytelling and the natural loyalty in Semitic family systems, cultural mores, and patterns of action, values and goals were transmitted from Fathers to sons (Genesis 22: 27, 37).

A further example can be seen in Moses with Joshua. Joshua was chosen by Moses to serve him, which Joshua was more than willing to do. In Exodus 33:11, the bible states that Moses would commune with God in the tent, and Joshua would follow him. He heard the conversations between Moses and the Lord, no doubt learning to commune with the Lord as well... a key to his successful ministry. Moses was important to Joshua, but God's presence even more so, as he would remain in the Tent of Meeting after Moses departed (Exodus 33:11).

Eli the high priest had two sons, Phinehas and Hophni. The scripture describes them as "worthless men" who committed many abominable acts as priests (1 Samuel 2:12). Though Eli tried to rebuke them (v22), he lacked the courage to bring them to accountability and the results were disastrous. (1 Samuel 4:11, 18-22).

Elijah the Prophet chose Elisha, a man of success, hard work, and means. He (Elijah) threw his "mantle" on him, signifying his choice as successor (1 Kings 20: 20-21). Elisha followed Elijah, ministering to Elijah, and inherited a double portion of Elijah's power for ministry (2 Kings 2: 9-10).

Our greatest example is seen in the ministry of Jesus Christ. Having prayed all night, Jesus chose from among many potential followers, twelve men to be with him (Luke 6:12-13).

From the moment Jesus chose his twelve, they followed him, observed him, emulated him, and learned from him necessary truths for life and ministry. By upbringing, all of these men (and the many women who followed Jesus) had culturally preconceived concepts of who Messiah would be, how he might minister, etc. However, all had to allow their theories to be tested in real practice; (Matthew 10, Luke 9) in the real world. Jesus mentored his disciples to be like him, and further to be like his Father in word and action.

The principle of discipleship or mentorship can be seen most clearly in the life and teaching of the Apostle Paul. Rejected by the church in Jerusalem, he was mentored by Barnabas (Acts 11), and he mentored Silas and Timothy (Acts 15:40, 16:1) and encouraged Timothy and all leaders under him to, from that time forward, find faithful men and women who could teach others the dynamic principles of God's word also (2 Timothy 2:2).

The process, of the more mature, gifted, and called men and women, mentoring or disciplining younger, less mature, less gifted men and women, has a strong tradition. However, one caution should be noted. Abraham and the patriarchs mentored their family who were proven loyal and faithful by blood. Moses, Elijah, Jesus and Paul heard from the Father before choosing their disciples. This was a supernatural or spiritual relationship, a knitting together of lives, for a greater purpose. Thus, mentor relationship should be entered into with care, much prayer, and for the benefit of both, and with a focus on fulfilling the purposes of the kingdom of God.

Fathers as Mentors

Training others is a basic work of the ministry. This was central to Paul's success. He instructed Timothy to take the things he had learned and to commit them to faithful men, who in turn would be able to teach others also (2 Timothy 2:2). This takes on even more importance when it is observed that Jesus spent a considerable amount of time and energy pouring himself into a relatively few individuals.

It should be noted that the Bible never actually speaks of Bible Schools as such. There are hints of 'schools of the prophets' (2

Kings 2:2-7). The teachers were not called 'teachers' and the students were not called 'students'. Our modern concepts of education and training come more from the Greeks than Hebrews. The students were called the 'sons' of the prophets and the prophets were regarded as 'fathers' (2 Kings 2:12).

The Old Testament view continued into the New Testament; a 'father' taking on a 'son', as he trained people in ministry. Without any doubt, this is the relationship of Paul and Timothy (Acts 16:1-4; Philippians 2:19-22; 1 Timothy 1:2; 2 Timothy 1:2; 2:1; 3:10-11) as well as Paul and Titus (Titus 1:4). It should become obvious that only those who have gained the heart of a father can become a successful mentor/coach. Without the father's heart coming through consistently, the younger men will feel 'used' instead of 'developed.'

This last point cannot be overemphasized. The power to influence, and to demand a following, comes from the heart of the leader, which expresses itself as a 'nursing mother', who cherishes her children with deep affection (1 Thessalonians 2:7-8) and as a 'father,' who exhorts, comforts and charges his own children (1 Thessalonians 2:11).

Who will young men follow? What characteristics do they need to see in a coach? What must they see before they will trust? Trust must be earned. A mentor or coach cannot demand trust unless his life is consistent, congruent with the message he heralds, reliable, and full of integrity. Young men called into ministry are not volunteers signing a contract; they are youthful men entering into a covenant relationship, trusting their very lives to another. They have to believe that the coach knows what he is doing.

Those in ministry must rise to the level of 'fathers' (1 John 2:12-14). As 'little children,' believers tend to relate everything to themselves; how they benefit from the actions of Christ. 'Young men' focus on the development of strength and authority, and overcoming the wicked one by the Word. 'Fathers' on the other hand, have the ability to see the heart and purpose of God.

'Fathers' are able to set an example that commands and inspires others to follow (Philippians 3:17; 4:9). A 'father' is someone who has gone beyond a general calling, choosing to be a bond slave. He has also progressed past his special calling, where his unique and particular gifting is developed normally, accompanied by rigorous pressure and privation. In addition to these, a 'father' enters the joy of begetting himself in others, of multiplying, imparting and extending his own spiritual life and vision to others who would likewise continue the stream. His own spirit, intensity and dedication are brought forth in others.

The example of Moses is sufficient to teach us that it is not enough just to be trained. Following the advice of his father-in-law, Moses trained and delegated responsibility to many leaders. However, that did not prevent his sense of aloneness in the work of the ministry, as Numbers 11:11-15 painfully reveals. Where were all the helpers that had been trained? The solution to Moses' dilemma was to have others receive of the Spirit that was upon him (Numbers 11:16-17, 25). This lesson points out that it is not enough to train and delegate: there must also be an impartation of spirit, from the man or woman of God, to his/her workers. We must ever be diligent to guard against 'methods' or 'formulas' that guarantee success. God does not use methods as much as he uses men and women. The methods and mannerisms of ministry are as many and as varied as the people God calls.

What kind of a coach/mentor should a leader seek to be? Unconsciously, all good leaders are mentoring others by way of example. Their lives inspire others to emulate and seek what they see evidenced in a seasoned man or woman of God. Sometimes the mentoring takes place on an occasional level, where advice is given to younger men and women to correct perspectives concerning themselves, circumstances and ministry. For instance, a teacher can share knowledge and insights on a particular subject. In addition to these kinds of mentoring, a man of God should be relating to some others on an intensive and intentional level, where through intimate relationships he disciples them, enabling them to minister effectively to others. He spiritually guides them by exhibiting accountability, providing direction and insight, and motivating them to bring their skills to meet the challenges of ministry.

As a 'father,' a mentor can see 'prophetically' more potential in others than the person sees in themselves. Because of that perspective, they will encourage the student to set demanding goals that cause the younger to stretch beyond what they feel they are capable of delivering, and they will assist them to make the decisions that will set the course of their lives. Through this means, the spiritual strengths of the younger are identified and attention can be applied to their weaknesses.

Some insight into the role of a father can be gleaned from the relationship Paul had with the Corinthians. He had begotten them through the gospel and was more than an instructor to them: he was a father to them, worthy of imitation (1 Corinthians 4:14-16). When this particular relationship was strained, Paul revealed the openness of his heart toward them (2 Corinthians 6:11-13). His heart was wide open to them, and he asks that they do the same in return (2 Corinthians 7:2).

How had Paul demonstrated his open heart towards his children at Corinth? He had lived his life courageously in taking the Gospel to them, and then they were well aware of what he was to them (2 Corinthians 5:20; 6:3-10). He explicitly informs them of his affection for them (2 Corinthians 6:11), a truth that had been demonstrated by his sacrifice in bringing the Gospel to them. In spite of their behavior, he still appealed to them as a father to his children (2 Corinthians 6:13). Today's Coaches/mentors can glean much from Paul's example.

The Example of Jesus

By studying the strategy of Jesus, we determine that he placed extreme importance in devoting himself to a few men. Some scholars suggest that half of his ministry time was spent with the few disciples, not the masses! The entire success of his mission upon earth hinged on the ability of these few men to carry it on after his departure. As he was about to go to the cross, where he offered his life as a ransom for many, his thoughts were mainly focused on these few men. Indeed, the whole world, for which he was about to die, did not receive as much attention as they were given. This is reflected in his prayer in the Garden of Gethsemane (John 17: 1-26, esp. v.9). He constantly referred to them in everything he did. Per John 17:20, the success of the Gospel rested with them. Thus, everything Jesus did, was for their sakes. He granted revelation (17:6), taught them (17:8, 14), prayed for them (17:9), kept them (17:12), shared glory with them (17:26), and sanctified himself for their benefit (17:19).

Therefore, Jesus' approach to ministry was to use people, not methods. His policy was to gather and then scatter. As their shepherd, Jesus gave his disciples personal and individual attention, leading them into ministry but not driving them. This should serve to emphasize the need of the teaching ministry over and above the miraculous. It would be the constant teaching that prepares men for the work of the ministry.

Jesus was a man of authority. He taught with authority (Matthew 7:29). This authority was hard won in the wilderness (Luke 4:14). His entire life was subjected to the will of the Father and everything about him was singly devoted to this purpose. He was a man with a mission, whose life spoke so loudly that it enticed others to devote themselves to the same great purpose. Coaches need credibility, or authority. It has been said that those who cannot do, teach. That certainly cannot be true for a coach, any more than it was for Jesus.

Jesus was highly skilled in his craft. Before his public ministry, he was already recognized as an able Rabbi (Luke 4:16). As a master teacher, he employed various means of communication through which he trained his followers: nurturing, teaching to impart, establishing true discipleship, building relationships, setting the pace, edifying and exhorting them. He realized that men's character is built by faithfulness over a period of time.

What, then, are the principles Jesus followed to ensure the success of the ministry in these men? How can we, who are called to coach others from Christian principles, do so effectively? How can there be an impartation of call, anointing and lifestyle to others? In other words, how can a dedicated Christian coach duplicate him or herself and multiply ministry in others? As the work of God grows and expands, the one who first received the call to do it becomes physically unable to embrace all of it. How is this resolved? – By mentoring others with the heart of a 'father.'

Mentoring/Coaching Begins by Prayerful Selection

In Jesus ministry, he invited many to follow him who listened to his teachings. John, Andrew, Peter, Philip, and Nathaniel had all previously met him (John 1:35-51). Jesus called to ministry both James (Mark 1:19; Matthew 4:21) and Matthew (Mark 2:13-14; Matthew 9:9; Luke 5:27-33). At first, they were part of a much larger group.

As time went on, Jesus sought for 'the twelve' his Father would give him. Out of the multitude, he selected a few. He once sent out seventy with supernatural power (Luke 10:1-17). But this number proved to be too large for effective mentoring. Finally he chose twelve, a manageable number for intimate training. Upon these few hinged the work of the ministry after Jesus physically departed this world.

Thus, no doubt, he spent much time in communion with his Father in the selection of these men. Alone with God in the mountains, he perceived which men the Father would give to him (Luke 6:12-16). He called them to be with him (quality and quantity of time are both important, Matthew 10:1-4). Of these twelve, three were given greater attention than the others and had even further access to the private side of Jesus (Mark 5:37; 9:2; 14:33; Luke 8:51).

What kind of men did Jesus choose? What qualifications were needed to carry on the mighty work of the kingdom of heaven? On face value, Jesus did not pick the right class of men. Politically and socially, these twelve were poles apart. They were not rich, they were not poor... in fact, they were middle class, with time to pursue the offer of Jesus to become fishers of men. The gospels reveal that they were a fractious group: ambitious, argumentative, prejudiced, impulsive, temperamental, and easily offended. They were ordinary men, without any formal training (Acts 4:13). On one occasion, Jesus denied them the pleasure of calling down fire on those who slighted them.

These twelve were deliberately chosen (John 6:70). With determination to make the proper selections, Jesus showed no haste in selecting these twelve. Jesus took time to observe the people he would eventually choose to follow him. In spite of what was seen on the surface, Jesus was guided by prophetic insight, as revealed by his comments in John 1:35-51 to Peter and Nathaniel.

Many times Jesus had to be patient with the disciples (e.g. Matthew 17:17). Perhaps the main attribute of these men was their sincere willingness to learn. His followers generally had hoped for the Messiah (John 1:41, 45, 49; 6:69), but some had already followed the Baptist (John 1:35).

After selecting the twelve, Jesus continued his public ministry at large (Mark 6:31 etc.), but he did not put his trust in the crowds as a means of success (John 2:23-25; John 6:26). Obviously, Jesus did not want the kingdom of heaven to be built upon popularity (a lesson modern preachers must learn!) and avoided undue publicity (Mark 1:44; 3:11-12; 5:43; 8:25-26; Matthew 9:30). The kingdom of heaven is not founded on sensationalism, and Jesus would often slip away from the crowds immediately after a miracle (John 6:14-15; Mark 4:35-36; 6:1; 45-46; 7:24; Matthew 8:18; 14:22; 15:39; Luke 5:15-16). Stability is not built on the fickleness of crowds. Many saw miracles, but very few understood them.

The goal of Jesus was not to impress people, become popular, or create a sensation. His purpose was to establish the kingdom of God. To do this, key men were needed. Leadership had to be developed in order to minister to the masses (Mark 6:34; Matthew 9:36; 14:14). Yet the foundation for such a ministry cannot be constructed on those masses. Large groups of humanity can be inspired easily and they can be disillusioned rapidly (Matthew 21:1-11 and 27:20-23). Human nature is capricious. Victory is won by the few, not the multitudes. Training leadership is slow and tedious, but necessary.

Jesus wanted a few men. What was his primary purpose in leading them? What would be their first lesson? It was simply to be with Jesus before anything else (Mark 3:13-19).

Coaching by Association

Knowledge is gained by association. Jesus called the disciples to himself (Luke 6:13). He required his disciples to be with him before he would send them out to preach (Mark 3:14). Having been with Jesus from the beginning, they would be effective witnesses (John. 15:27).

There were no formal schools, seminaries or outlined study materials. Preparation for ministry came by a mentor-student relationship. It is a biblical principle that the work is bound up in the worker. Therefore, the best way for a learner to understand the work is to be intimately associated with the worker. It is apprenticeship, not scholasticism. The worker himself is the school of learning.

Adhering to the command "Follow me" is the method of learning (Mark 1:17). The mentor himself is the lesson to be taught and the passion to be caught. Coaching uses different skills, but with similar goals in mind.

Association communicates knowledge and purpose first. Doctrine comes by discipleship (John 18:19). Understanding comes as a result of intimate fellowship, as a development of knowledge gained by association. The invitation of a mentor is first to "Come and see" (John 1:39, 46), "Follow me" (John 1:43; Mark 2:14; Matthew 9:9; Luke. 5:27), and "Come after me" (Mark 1:17; Matthew 4:19; Luke. 5:10). As already stated, the lessons are bound up in the life of the worker and mentor.

As time passed, Jesus gave increasingly intimate attention to the twelve. He made many trips alone with his disciples. He took them along to Tyre and Sidon (Mark 7:24; Matthew 15:21), Decapolis (Mark 7:31; Matthew 15:29), Dalmanutha (Mark 8:10; Matthew 15:39), and Caesarea Philippi (Mark 8:27: Matthew 16:13). Part of this was due to the hostility of his enemies, but it was also to be alone with his disciples (John 11:54). He often took his disciples aside (Matthew 20:17; Mark 10:32). Growth in understanding came by association (John 16:4).

Jesus gave considerable personal attention to many people such as Zacchaeus (Luke 19:1-10), the Samaritans (John 4:39-42), Bartimaeus (Mark 10:32), the seventy (Luke 10:1-17), and many faithful women (Luke 10:38-42). However, most of his time was devoted to the few the Father had given to him. They were the ones who were with him through the trials (Luke 22:28-30).

Jesus had great gifts, and the infinite wisdom of God, and he worked primarily with 12-70. It should be noted, some professional counselors can and do carry a case load (50 minutes per week or so per client) of over 30, some coaches do as well. However, the ideal seems to be about 12-20 clients per week. This is a realistic number to work with.

Mentoring and the Requirement of Obedience (or Commitment to a Covenant)

Jesus expected loyalty and obedience. A disciple is a learner, a pupil. To be mentored, one must pay a price. The terms of discipleship were laid out in no uncertain terms. Surrender of life in absolute submission is a prerequisite. The cost must be counted (Luke 14:25-35); sin must be forsaken; love must be perfected; and obedience must be demonstrated. Obedience is the proof of love (John 14:15, 21, 23, 24; 15:10-12). This obedience had been fully demonstrated by Jesus (John 4:34; 5:30; 6:38; 17:4; Luke 22:42; Mark 14:36; Matt 26:39). The disciples would become more like Jesus through obedience to him. If those being mentored witness obedience in the Master, they will follow suit.

The reason for this is simple. Learning comes by obedience and doing. The disciples had left all to follow Jesus (Matthew 19:27; Mark 10:28; Luke 18:28). Defects in their character would be dealt with as they grew in grace and knowledge. There is always a cost to grow...remember, if something is free, it doesn't mean much...thus is true in life and coaching...thus a fee is appropriate, even necessary. It establishes commitment.

Coaching by Imparting

The coach/mentor is continuously giving his or her services away. More than just our expertise, our life is imparted to others. Jesus constantly gave the same to his disciples (John 15:5; 17:4, 8, 14). *

- He gave his peace (John 16:33)
- He gave joy (John 15:11; 17:13),
- He gave the keys of the kingdom (Matthew 16:19; Luke 12:32)
- He gave glory (John 17:22, 24).

Love constantly gives out (John 15:13). People responded to Jesus because of his continuous giving out.

The most revealing things were taught only to the chosen few disciples (Matthew 11:27; 13:10-11; 16-17; 16:17; Mark 4:10-11; Luke 8:9-10; 10:22). Jesus invested all he had into the few.

This continuous imparting of the mentor becomes the basis of ministry for those who are learning. They will give as they have received (Matthew 10:8); and love as they have been loved (John 13:34-35).

The mentor will cause his followers to be dependent upon the Holy Spirit, because they will one day be released from His physical presence. Therefore, the mentor will demonstrate ministry in the power of the Holy Spirit and lead others into a dynamic relationship with the Holy Spirit. It is the Holy Spirit who makes the difference, not the natural boastings of a man.

Coaching by Visibility and Demonstration

Jesus said, "I have given you an example that you should do as I have done unto you." (John 13:15). In addition to the washing of feet, this is true of many things about Jesus in his role of mentor. Perhaps the greatest lesson Jesus visibly demonstrated in episodes such as the washing of feet was that a servant's demeanor precipitates true, influential leadership.

*Although there is no record of Jesus receiving "tuition" from his disciples, it was common practice for disciples to contribute to their missions from their private means.

The Gospel of Luke especially shows the prayer life of Jesus (Luke 3:21; 6:12; 9:18,29; 10:21-22; 22:32,39-46 – see also Matthew 26:27; John 17:6-19). It is important to note here that the disciples were able to observe the prayer life of the Master, their Mentor. It caused them to learn to do the same (Luke 11:1-13).

The same is true with regard to the Master's use of scripture. He constantly talked of it when he was with his disciples. No less than sixty-six references to scriptures are found in Jesus' discourses with the disciples.

Jesus constantly took advantage of every circumstance, turning it into a teaching moment. Unaware that learning was taking place, the disciples were always absorbing some lesson. The message, though its outline may not have been prepared in advance, naturally unfolded in conversation.

Much was taught by way of example. Because of their close association, the disciples could inquire further into anything that they did not fully understand. Often the explanation was more intense than the original teaching they heard; as shown in the parables of the kingdom (Matthew 13). Sometimes Jesus would initiate the expanded lesson to the disciples (Matthew 9:23-20:16; Mark 10:24-31; Luke 18:25-30). When Jesus taught in the synagogue, the presentation was formal. When he taught the crowds, he gave broad concepts, often in parables; however, for the committed followers, there was more intimate knowledge in the form of clear, plain and specific instructions and explanations.

It is well worth noting that the ministry of Jesus is first 'doing' before teaching (Acts 1:1). This is not the usual method of the rabbis who first taught and then did. Example was set, and much learning came from doing. Vision must first be 'caught' and then real teaching may begin (Matthew 16:16, 21). All else is preliminary.

Everything Jesus taught was demonstrated in his life, showing and proving its workability. By example, 'class' was always in session. What the disciples were to learn was constantly lived before them. This was also evident in the life of Paul (1 Corinthians 11:1; 1 Thessalonians 1:5-6; 2:7; Philippians 3:17; 4:9; 2 Timothy 1:13). When knowledge is not applied to living, it can become a stumbling block to future growth.

Coaching by Delegation or Activation

At first, the disciples were simply called to be with Jesus, more observers than workers. They could witness how the mentor worked. Even after ordination, they did little during the first year except to watch, to comprehend his vision and activity. Then they were given work to do, as they could handle it.

Their first responsibilities were most likely simple. They arranged things such as accommodation and food (John 4:8). They were involved early in assisting with baptizing people (John 4:2). Elisha first became a servant to Elijah before receiving his mantle (1 Kings 19:21). Joshua was referred to in the beginning as the assistant of Moses (Exodus 24:13). Eventually Moses laid hands on Joshua (Numbers 27:1823) with the result that Joshua was filled with the spirit of wisdom for leadership (Deuteronomy 34:9).

It was not until the third year that Jesus began to involve his disciples directly with his tours of ministry (Matthew 9:3-10:1ff; Mark 6:6-7ff; Luke 9:1-2). As observed in these scriptures, instructions that were observed implicitly earlier were then expounded explicitly.

There was a definite purpose to Jesus methodology. The task was clarified. The urgency and immediacy of the mission was stressed (Matthew 10:7). The spiritual authority and gifts they were to use were outlined (Matthew 10:8). They were given specific instructions concerning where to go (Matthew 10:6-7); indeed, they were sent to those who would receive their ministry. An emphasis was also added about the provision for a place of faith (Matthew 10:8-10). They were instructed to stay with people who were worthy, not with those who were not (Matthew 10:11-14; Mark 6:10; Luke 9:4). In this way, they would establish a 'beachhead.' They were to expect hardship and opposition and even persecution, but they were to rely completely on the Holy Spirit in every circumstance (Matthew 10:17-32) and to recall the example of Jesus in these things (Matthew 10:24-25).

Before sending the disciples out, Jesus shared his authority and power with them (Matthew 10:1; Mark 6:7; Luke 9:1; see also Matthew 10:40; John 13:20).

It is significant that Jesus sent them out in pairs (Mark 6:7-12; Luke 9:2-6). He also did this with the larger group of seventy followers (Luke 10:1-17). Not only did they minister the kingdom of God, but also acted as forerunners of Jesus, preparing the way for him.

The disciples now had a definite command. That which was received by impulse at the beginning of their discipleship had been progressively clarified and made specific. This works with coaching as well.

Coaching by Supervision

Jesus often asked probing questions of his disciples as a means of review and instruction. By doing this, he challenged and stretched their faith (Mark 8:16-21). After a mission had been fulfilled, Jesus would hear their reports, as in the case of the seventy (Luke 10:17).

There seems to have been an alteration between assignments and reports.

In these times, Jesus rejoiced in their news (Luke 10:18, 21-22). He asked questions, gave illustrations, and issued admonitions (Luke 10:18-20). Apparently, previous arrangements had been made for the disciples to report to Jesus what they did and taught (Mark 6:30; Luke 9:10). It is also significant in these verses that Jesus immediately took them away for rest.

These check-up sessions were used for new teaching, instruction, review and application. There were many occasions when Jesus spoke with his disciples after an incident, such as their failure to cast out an evil spirit (Mark 9:17-29; Matthew 17:14-20; Luke 9:37-43), or their bewilderment at the feeding of the multitudes (Matthew 14:13-21; 15:29-38; Mark 6:30-44; 8:1-21; Luke 9:10-17; John 6:1-13). In the midst of these circumstances, Jesus stretched their faith and insights. He was able to exemplify his teachings using particular life circumstances.

Finally – Reproduction

In choosing the few into whom he would pour his life, the goal of Jesus was to cause them to bear fruit (John 15:16). Through this mentoring process, a structure had been built into these men that would challenge and triumph as his prayer in John 17:20-23 reflects. After his physical departure, these disciples, relying on the Holy Spirit, were to be sent out (John 20:21-23).

"As they go out, they now will make disciples of other men" (Matthew 28:19-20; Mark 16:15).

All of this shows that Jesus followed a deliberate plan in mentoring others; the same applies to ministries today. To meet the growing need, men of God today need to duplicate themselves by the process of mentoring. We need coaches who will utilize the methods of Jesus to help others grow into their God sized destinies.

What is Mentoring/Coaching?

Before looking more specifically at coaching/mentoring, a view from the top might help. From God's (the Bible) perspective, every human being, regardless of circumstance of birth is precious to him. In Psalm 139:13, the Psalmist, inspired by the Holy Spirit states;

> "For you formed my inward parts; you knitted me together in my mother's womb. I praise you for I am fearfully and wonderfully made."

We are created in the image and likeness of God (Genesis 1:26-28) and are thus of infinite worth to God. In fact, he loved us so much that he sent Jesus to die on a cross, so that we could experience the forgiveness of sin and an abundant life here, followed by eternal life in the Fathers family. Thank God.

Thus, as a Christian Life Coach, our view of mankind, contrary to the sin or sickness model (look for what is wrong), we, like God, look to bring to the present and future all the gifts, abilities goals and dreams of our client to the forefront. This is for their benefit and others, and ultimately for the glory of God. As a counselor or therapist, my focus is to find the area of sin, emotional blockage or stinking thinking that keeps my client from experiencing the Kingdom of God and an abundant life; righteousness peace and joy in the Holy Spirit.

The focus was the past and the deficits in thinking or behavior in the person due to nature or nurture. With coaching, our focus is more on the present and future, with a strong emphasis on faith, vision, dreams, goals and values leading to a brighter and more prosperous future. Rather than a healing emphasis, it is a training, equipping, guiding, encouraging ministry. Both healing and equipping may be needed in a client; wisdom is knowing what emphasis is needed and when.

Mentoring has been defined as the dynamic activity of assisting another; giving of advice from a trusted adviser. In a similar way, coaching is done by a person who is a private tutor or a trainer, such as one would see in athletics, with a goal of teaching or training privately, for more effective performance.

The role of a coach or mentor is to assist an individual or a group to maximize and utilize their skills and abilities to fulfill a mission. The mission, whether it is a team sport, personal growth, climbing the corporate ladder or achieving a noble ministry objective, is to be defined by the student/disciple and the coach/mentor, according to agreed upon core values. As Christians, our core values are to be extrapolated from God's manual for faith and service; the Bible. However, it is not the laws of scripture that motivate us towards a mission, but the principles of the Word, summarized by Jesus as "loving the Lord our God with all our heart, soul, mind and strength, and our neighbor as ourselves."

In practical outworking, mentoring/coaching is a relationship built on trust and shared expertise, on common goals and honest desire, to achieve excellence. In brief, the key components to successful mentoring/coaching include:

- Vision – Vision requires a thorough knowledge of God's intentions for the world and our specific role in it.
- Mission – Our mission flows from our Vision, and must be consistent with our calling.
- Core Values – As determined by our life priorities, by God's word and by our behavioral or Personality style.
- Purpose – The working out of the meaning of our purpose is vital to happy and healthy living. Our purpose must be clearly defined.
- Action Plans – the actual plan of action should follow our goals; and be in keeping with our purposes, core values, mission and vision.

- Life Evaluation – Mentoring often requires mid-course adjustment; requiring honesty, openness, vulnerability, communication, mutual respect and accountability.

In coaching, this is a time - limited process, but one, we hope, which will induce a desire for continual growth and development for God's glory.

"If you have a dream, don't just sit there. Gather courage to believe that you can succeed and leave no stone unturned to make it a reality."

Roopleen

"Seek opportunities to show you care. The smallest gestures often make the biggest difference."

John Wooden

Chapter 14:
Getting Down to It: How Can Coaching Help?

Coaching focuses on the positive. Healthy change in both leader and follower is possible through professional coaching. Starting from committed, trusting relationships, using probing questions which lead to insight, goals and strategy, coaches bless their clients with their willingness to listen, confront and care.

Coaching can help in several areas of a fellow believer's life. The helping process is relationally based, where trust is essential. The specific steps to helping a coachee are presented here in a somewhat simple, but workable way, in our ABCD model.[8]

Achieve a Relationship: We can assist a person in reaching their goals and dreams only if they trust us. Thus, achieving a relationship is essential. This begins with being a friendly, personable person, with a purpose of developing a short or long term agreement for the coach to journey with the coachee for mutual benefit. Again, building a relation of trust is key, requiring strong listening skills filled with empathy, warmth and respect.

Boil Down the Goals: Boiling down a person's vision and dream, and helping them to focus on what is most important for their life now and for the future takes skill. As a coach, you are to encourage the coachee to articulate their goals and dreams, their vision and purposes. This is to be done preferably in writing, and must include the timeframe for your work together, the key values the client is working from, and your mutual agreement to work towards stated goals.

---

[8] Adapted from my book, Crisis Counseling, by Vision Publishing, www.booksbyvision.com

Confront in love: As a coach, you will be asking questions that will help the coachee face areas of their lives where their stated values are in conflict, goals and plans are off track, etc. Confrontation does not have to be harsh at all, but we are, as with all believers' to speak the truth in love, and help them face the truth which will set them on a right path.

Develop a Strategic Plan: All plans for the present and future are to be co-developed by the coach and the coachee. The plan, again, must be in keeping with values as previously discussed, and must be flexible. Blessed are the flexible, they shall not be broken!

Asking the Right Questions

Much of the coaching process is developed by asking key and sometimes difficult questions.

When I first meet with a client, I often ask "getting to know you" questions, such as:

- What is your goal for our meeting?
- What timeframe do you think will be necessary to see change happen in your life?
- What would you say are your core values and how are you living them out?
- Are you committed to working together at least 3 months? Are you willing to pay the price (including my fee)?

Coaches, mentors and counselors, though their goals and processes may be and should be different, this beginning of a professional relationship starts in similar ways.

First, there is a social phase… how are you? Any trouble finding my office? Tell me about your history (in brief)… leading to popping the question; how can I help you? Or what do you expect from our relationship?

From listening to the clients dreams and life story, goals and proposes emerge. The coaches' role, like a counselor, is to utilize in this early phase active listening skills without judgment. During this process the coach asks questions to clarify, and to create greater understanding and trust.

Remember, in coaching we are not looking for a lifelong commitment, but commitment to the process for certain. It is assumed that Jesus' disciples came to him with hat in hand (no money). But this is highly unlikely. As a teacher (Rabbi), it was traditional to receive tuition for study, a contribution to the cause, thus the need for a common purse. The concept of implied value is as ancient as time. If coaching is free, it must not be worth much. Charging per a person's ability to pay or on occasion accepting a low fee client may be fine, but good coaching should cost something. Your time, your expertise, your training, your commitment and work deserves compensation. Though our approach to coaching is distinctively Christian, our work is not free, as the laborer is worthy of hire. Questions regarding commitment on both sides must be clear and clearly answered.

There are many ways to structure the discovery and pursuing of one's life purpose. We're going to organize the search with a model called the Seven Life Purpose Questions. By focusing around these seven themes, we will help coaches understand where the process is going, and how the different pieces of the puzzle fit together.

The seven questions are:

1. Whose, am I? That is, do I belong to myself, my parents, spouse, employer, God…and what does that mean in terms of relationships, etc.

2. Who am I? Our identity, initiially formulated developmentally in our family of origin, goes beyond our self esteem, but certainly encompasses it. How do we feel about ourselves, our gifts, our abilities, and who defines for us who we are…the culture, our relative success, God and his word, etc. Very important question.

3. What has my life, experiences, etc., prepared me for? As one looks back, what do they see and how do they interpret their life experiences.

4. Why do I want coaching? This is important as the focus of coaching is client centered.

5. Where is God in the process of my life? This goes beyond religious affiliation, church attendance, etc., but may well include these. It is more the question of does God and the bible inform or give input to decisions in life, and to what degree?

6. When will I begin to see my life, full and fulfilled? The client must ultimately define what success is for them, and part of the coaches' responsibility is to help them make and work towards achieving their goals or destiny.

7. How will I get there? I have found that most people I coach have a general idea about how to get to where they want to go, but often lack motivation, or information necessary, or in some cases the courage to act out a plan. Good coaching addresses these potential issues effectively.

Finding Your Lifestyle

How do you help a client align with the lifestyle of their call? Our sample dialog illustrates a step-by-step process. This is from an actual coaching session with a strong Christian leader named George.

First, after getting to know each other a bit, we discussed George's call. We came to the conclusion that his current life circumstances were not an obstacle to that call, but were exactly what was needed to fulfill it. Finally, we discussed George's expectations for his lifestyle, and what if any changes would need to be made to fulfill his call and ultimate life purpose.

The key to this technique is the assumption that all of life flows toward one's destiny, and that God sovereignly leverages every circumstance to that end. That is a powerful combination for reframing: "if you are called, and your circumstances are intentionally moving you toward that call, then what does the fact that you are here now mean?"

What alerts the coach to the need to reframe is the dissonance between George's stated objective, (to walk the walk of leaders who are struggling financially) and his expectations (that he would quickly enjoy financial success). George thought he would help his leaders best by succeeding and showing them how to succeed. The coach offered another potential perspective: that a straighter road to his objective might be available.

Creating a Growth Plan

Once you have reviewed the assessment together, you are ready to start planning how to explore the coaching plan. Gathering information in the beginning about the coachee is useful as you move forward. I find it wise to use the forms in the appendix, and insist that the client complete them fully and that we discuss them completely. This also holds true if I utilize a DISC profile... it is not just good information to store as historical data, but is to be used in the coaching process.

Remember, with different clients there are different seasons of life, therefore we need different levels of life purpose insight. Some may just want to learn enough to make a better career decision the next month, while others are seeking to realign their whole lives around an ultimate purpose.

To maintain high buy-in, involve the client as much as possible in creating the growth plan. Here are three possible approaches:

Ask for a Strategy

Ask coachees to identify where they need to grow based on the assessment, and then solicit options and steps that translate those goals into actions.

While this option does a good job of keeping ownership with the client, it does not always work. The challenge is that the client may not know where the opportunities for growth are, let alone how to effectively pursue them.

To make a wise decision, you must have a certain amount of information about the alternatives. These days, you would not want to buy a new car without finding out the gas mileage it will get. In the same way, a client is going to need a certain amount of information about possible options to make good decisions. You have a set of life purpose tools the client does not know about (the options). So, unless your client is self-aware or has already done a fair amount of destiny work, you are going to have to provide that information for the client to make a wise decision. Our second possible approach is:

Present Options

Come to an agreement on the areas to focus on, present several tools that could move things forward. Ask the coachee to choose which one(s) seem most compelling.

Strengths and Personality Type

Thirdly, a survey of strengths and personality types can lead to a coaching plan. Strengths, and personality types have much in common because inward mechanisms and outward performance are connected. However, strengths can describe things that don't fit well under personality type ("he's really good with his hands" or "she picks up languages easily"), whereas personality types often explain inner functions that are not strengths (for example, as will be discussed in depth under "Understanding your Style; a "D's" root fear is loss of control and being taken advantage of). At the far left end of strengths are the purely physical qualities that are not part of our personality at all, like hand-eye coordination. The right end of the spectrum features things like core motivations or a desire for privacy that are not strengths or weaknesses, but simply portray our individuality. We might say that personality types describe our inner workings, while strengths describe aptitudes for doing certain things. For instance, a "C" on the DISC™ is inwardly motivated to do things right and bring them to completion (their type), which tends to give them an aptitude for jobs like accounting that requires precision with numbers (a strength).

Both personality types and strength systems create sorting categories that offer the language to understand human differences. I find it most helpful to view these categories as continuums with fuzzy boundaries. Some clients (particularly "C's" on the DISC™) can get sidetracked by trying to make sure every insight into their purpose is placed in the "right" category. Their insights are real; the categories are simple artificial constructs that help us remember and understand the insights. Whether something is a 'strength' or a 'type', quality is much less important than just knowing it is there!

Strengths vs. Skills

Sometimes clients confuse strengths and skills. A skill is the practiced ability to do a task well. It is proficiency. However, it is possible to be proficient in something that does not come naturally! Many clients seek coaching because they can do their jobs well but don't enjoy them; or they can succeed at the tasks assigned to them but feel sucked dry by the extraordinary effort it takes to do so. Skills are not always strengths. This helps surface the degree of alignment between role and strengths, and suggests where changes might be made to better utilize strengths. I like to mate this exercise with a personality assessment, since it provides another layer of information about the ideal role. Normally, these exercises are done as personal reflections between coaching appointments. Encourage your clients to e-mail you their work beforehand – it is much easier to coach around the exercise when you have it in hand and have had the chance to review it. When I'm looking at a client's strengths list, I'm scanning for outstanding insights to affirm, obstacles to functioning in one's strengths, whether the person is truly identifying strengths (and not learned skills or something else), and how able the individual is to name strengths and weaknesses.

One way to help those who are not as adept at reflection is to work through one's strength in your session as an example. Use the exercise questions until one 'strength' is identified, and then turn them loose to find the rest. For instance, if you are doing the Strengths Inventory, ask: "Give me an example. What is one of your best strengths?" Those who can name and unpack a strength can probably finish up on their own. With those who can't, you have a chance to troubleshoot before they waste a week being stuck.

Some people struggle to name strengths because they are unreflective or simply not self-aware. What I like to do in these cases is to start with past successes and failures to find the strengths and weaknesses within those experiences.

Identify Strengths Behind the Successes

Now take each of the successes or accomplishments in turn. Which of the talents and abilities does this story highlight? What did the client bring to the table that made this a success? Which parts came naturally, or had a big impact, with what felt like little effort? Some questions to reveal strengths include:

"What did you do that made this thing succeed?"

"What skills were needed to do this?"

"Which part energized you or came naturally to you?"

"What did you see or do in the situation that others could not or would not?"

"What did others affirm in you when you accomplished this?"

"What did you do that made the most difference with the least effort?"

Helping the client to understanding their inherent and historical strengths can help them to have courage to launch forward to new successes in the future.

Dream Principles

Martin Luther King's "I Have a Dream" speech illustrates a number of important dreaming principles we can apply to the life coaching process. Take a moment to reread the speech to fix it in your mind, and then we'll dive in.[9]

Dreams are Visual Images

Notice the abundant imagery in King's Speech. He carries you to "the red hills of Georgia," to a future where "little black boys and girls will be able to join hands with little white boys and girls and walk together as brothers." You don't hear King's speech so much as you see it. Visual images affect us much more deeply and are more powerfully motivating than words. Therefore, we will encourage clients to use the process of visualization to turn the skeleton of important dreams into fleshed-out pictures thus helping them to envision then dream and begin working towards them Envisioning Your Dream.

Dreams Reveal Deep Desires

King's dream touches us at a visceral, emotional level because it expresses the heart-cry of an entire people for freedom and justice. Dreams are like that: they resonate with the passions of our hearts. One service to provide clients is to help them find the deep desires that lie beneath their dreams.

Values Characteristics

Core values are deeply held, enduring beliefs, that define what is most valuable or important to us. Often for clients seeking coaching, values can be in conflict. For example, a client tells you that his highest priority is his family, but in actuality, he spends nearly every weekend working, and spends little time with his spouse or children, causing undo pressure in the home. Below are a few characteristics defining what values are and are not.

---

[9] https://www.archives.gov/files/press/exhibits/dream-speech.pdf

Values are:

- Passionate - They define what you care most about and why you do what you do.
- Unique - Since they come from your heart, they're in your own words.
- Assumed - Values are so much a part of us that we forget that they are there.
- Lived - If you truly value something, your behavior demonstrates it.
- Lasting - Values don't change easily; they're deeply rooted in you.
- Values are not:
- Goals - Goals are committed future aims. Values are what you hold dear now.
- Aspirations - A value is something you already live, not what you aspire to.
- Principles - Values are not cause and effect statements of how life works, like "You reap what you sow"
- Doctrinal Statements - "I believe the Bible is the inerrant word of God" is a doctrinal statement, not a value.
- Visions - Values are rooted in the now; visions are pictures of an ideal future.

Four Characteristics of Great Value Statements

Short: One sentence, one phrase, or even a single word to keep it memorable.

"Now, can you sum that up in one sentence?"

"Can you shorten that into some pithy, meaningful phrases that can be unpacked?"

Unique: in your words, not someone else's.

"The language you are using could be true of a lot of people. Can you say that in a way that captures what is unique about you?"

"Can you say that in a way that if your friends read it, they'd know it was you?"

Un-packable: Every word and phrase has meaning.

"Unpack that for me – what does each phrase mean to you?"

"Take the key words there and tell me what each one means?"

Now: Written in the present tense, to describe who you are.

"How well is this statement reflected in your life right now?"

"Is that a value that you are living out already, or is it something you aspire to, that we might set a goal to reach?

It can be readily observed that men and women with consistent, lived out core values live happier and more fulfilling lives. Values in conflict is one area of life that increases stress and decreases efficiency in all areas of life.

How Does Coaching Help Leaders?

Sponsoring meaningful work: Coaching focuses consistent attention on providing people with the opportunity to experience meaningful work, regardless of title or position. Leaders, more than anyone, are hungry for meaning beyond meeting shareholder or bottom line targets. Leaders are interested in leaving a legacy that will make a positive difference in their world. Coaches pay attention to these questions and provide a sounding board for leaders to explore the issues and find solutions that make sense to them. Leaders who grapple with these questions create an environment for others to do the same, and eventually the organization's culture transforms.

Looking in the mirror: Coaching allows leaders to be self-reflective at the most difficult times. By exploring the leader's part in the complexity of issues such as employee turnover, diminishing market share, or lack of investor confidence, the coach assists the leader to reclaim personal power through his own vulnerability. The leader's own journey into the dark then becomes a beacon for others in the organization who are experiencing external pressure and who would otherwise have nowhere to express it.

Implementing wise decision making: Coaching takes strategic decision-making up a notch by inviting leaders to consider all the implications, rather than focusing on the urgent or the expedient. While this may appear to be a slower process, it actually results in decisions that have more positive long term effects, and thus require less re-work or re-consideration.

Focusing on long term viability: Lessons from the internet explosion apply equally to other organizations. Coaching can assist leaders to avoid the same pitfalls by using a clearly articulated long term vision as a touchstone for ongoing initiatives. The coach's approach to strategic planning makes room for the people factor that ultimately determines the success or failure of an organization.

Initiating courageous communication: Coaches model telling the truth in a way that makes room for new learning. The impact of global conditions since 9/11 and the continuing war in Afghanistan results in an increased need for the truth to be expressed by everyone in the workplace. Leaders are being called on to model truth-telling, and working with a coach gives them a place to practice for the high-risk environment outside their office doors.

Taking the best from the worst: An organization's stories are its lifeblood. Coaching draws a story from the most damaging situations and assists leaders to first see the gold for themselves, and then to share that learning with the organization.

Practicing what is preached: People take their cues from what leaders do more than from what they say. For an organization to create a team-based culture, the leadership must model what a high functioning team looks like. To break through habits of 'silo thinking,' and to shift from reward systems that focus on individual achievement to collective achievement, requires skill and dedication. Coaching provides feedback to executive teams that bring dysfunctional interactions to light and co-creates strategies for breaking habits that no longer serve the organization.

People are dying at their desks because they are afraid of the darkness that hides under the desk. Coaches earn the right to be companions on the journey into the dark places – where leaders and people at all levels of organizations find themselves – because of their commitment to face their own darkness. Coaches and their clients come out the other side with courageous lifelong learning, marked by lasting concrete results.

Conclusion:
Heart, Head and Hands

Ken Blanchard and friends use the term heart, head and hands in relation to collaborative leadership...and coaching certainly requires collaboration, working together to accomplish a specific obtainable goal. This is not a new concept, though not framed as nicely as Dr. Blanchard, and can be found in the writing of the Apostle Paul in 1 Timothy 1:5.

> "For the goal of our instruction is love, from a pure heart, and a good conscience, and a sincere faith." (NAS)

Writing to his son in the Lord, Timothy, Paul would have put much thought into his words. Every father wants his son or daughter to be successful, even more so than themselves. Thus, with great care and filled with love and concern, Paul reminds Timothy of the goal... of instruction, teaching, training or coaching. It all starts with the heart.

The heart or the center of the persons being must be changed if they are to be all that they can be. Paul states that it (our hearts) must be filled with love, agape' love. This is provided to us through the grace of God because we have been cleansed by Christ. This is both event and an ongoing process for all of us. Where there is darkness, light must shine, where we are missing the mark, we must refocus to achieve our goals...these are mainly heart issues, our values, deepest hopes and dreams. Paul does not stop there, but continues to the mind (which must be renewed in all of us, Romans 12:1,2). A good conscience does not mean guilt free (but would include it), but the ability to see things from God's perspective (the 30,000 foot perspective). A good or godly conscience does not deny problems or potential threats, but faces them in faith, knowing that God is with us. We have the mind of Christ, and as we grow we begin to think more like him.

Finally, Paul reminds Timothy that his behavior, his hands, matter as well. A faithful faith, or living from our principled heart and committed to Christ mindedness we act in concert with our core values. We are not like those tossed here and there because they will believe any teaching promising a quick fix or get rich quick scheme, but instead stay the course, following our transformed heart, our renewed mind with faithful actions.

A coach's life flows from a coached life. To be effective, we need coaches to help us become better coaches, as faithful men teach so others can be taught also. My hope is that you will pursue your coaching ministry with passion; and that you will have fruitful success for your benefit and God's glory.

Appendix:
Forms for Starting Your Work

- Vision – Vision requires a thorough knowledge of God's intentions for the world and our specific role in it. What is your vision for your life and future?

- Mission – Our mission flows from our Vision, and must be consistent with our calling. How would you define your mission for now and the future?

- Core Values – As determined by our life priorities, by God's word and by our behavioral or Personality style. List your top 5 core values and explain how you express them in your daily life and work.

- Purpose – The working out of the meaning of our purpose is vital to happy and healthy living. Our purpose must be clearly defined. Define yours.

- Action Plans – the actual plan of action should follow our goals; and be in keeping with our purposes, core values, mission and vision. What is your present plan of action, or if you do not have a clearly delineated one, what would you like it to be?

- Life Evaluation – Mentoring often requires mid-course adjustment; requiring honesty, openness, vulnerability, communication, mutual respect and accountability. Are you willing to pursue the process? How much time and energy are you willing to commit?

Coaching Contract

Client Name: _____

Date:_____

This agreement, between coach _____ and the above named client will begin on _____ and will continue for a period of _____ months, ending on _____.

Fees:

    The fee for the initial meeting is $_____ and the fee for the following meeting is $_____. These fees will be paid in advance.

    Alternatively, this is a _____ package for a period of _____ months, including _____ appointments per month for _____ minutes at a time.

    Additional appointments can be scheduled as needed. If you need to cancel an appointment, please provide at least 24 hour's notice or it will be necessary to charge you for the appointment time, as stated above.

Services:

    The services to be provided by the coach to the client are face-to-face or telephone-coaching, as agreed jointly with the client. Coaching may address specific personal projects, business successes, or general conditions in the client's life or profession. Other coaching services include value clarification, brainstorming, identifying plans of action, examining modes of operating in life, asking clarifying questions, and making empowering requests or suggestions for action.

    Throughout the working relationship, the coach will engage in direct and personal conversations. The client understands that successful coaching requires a co-active collaborative approach between client and coach. In the coaching relationship, the coach plays the role of a facilitator of change, but it is the client's responsibility to enact or bring about the change.

If the client believes the coaching is not working as desired, the client will communicate and take action to return the power to the coaching relationship.

Prior History

The client also agrees to disclose details of the past or present psychological or psychiatric treatment. Coaching and counseling are not the same and as such, there needs to be a clear distinction between the two.

Although I am a licensed Marriage and Family Therapist trained in counseling or therapy, I do not engage in therapy with my coaching clients. In entering into the coaching relationship, and signing the agreement, you are agreeing that if any mental health difficulties arise during the course of the coaching relationship, you will notify me immediately so that I can discuss with you an appropriate referral.

Privacy

The client can, at any point in the coaching session, declare his/her preference not to discuss a specific issue, by simply stating that they would rather not discuss this issue. The coach agrees to respect this boundary and will not attempt to forward the conversation further along those lines.

Confidentiality

The coach will work within the professional ethics and guidelines as designed by the International Coaching Federation (see www.coachfederation.org and www.aps.psychsociety.com.au). Copies of the ethical guidelines are available on the website. All information about the coach/client relationship will remain strictly confidential except in very rare circumstances where decreed by law; ie. where the court might issue a subpoena for the file or information.

If you wish for me as your coach to speak to someone outside our interactions, then you need to give me written permission (original letter, fax or email) to do so. Exceptions to confidentiality of course relate to circumstances such as intent to seriously harm someone, child abuse etc. Otherwise, all your information is confidential.

It is also important to note that in some situations, it is important to be aware of the use of technology in that for some clients, there is a risk in using certain media such as the internet, mobile phones and cordless phones. If you use these to communicate with me, then I will assume that it is appropriate to continue to do so in my interactions with you.

Termination

The coach and client agree to provide each other with two week's notice in the event it is desired to terminate coaching. Otherwise, the coaching will continue for the duration of the contracted period.

I believe that each of my clients is a unique, creative and responsible person who is in charge of moving their own life forward. I very much look forward to working with you.

Our signatures on this agreement indicate full understanding of and agreement with the information outlined above.

_____   _____

Coaching Client   Date

_____   _____

Executive & Personal Coach   Date

Life Review

As a Christian Life Coach, it is important to know who you are, what your strengths are and weaknesses. The purpose of this life review is to obtain a comprehensive picture of your background, as well, as a snapshot of where you are now. It may even help you identify areas that need work and it can reveal areas where you have overcome and walk in victory. This is simply a tool to help you.

If some particular question does not apply to you, simply write "N/A."

Today's Date: _____

General Information

Name: _____

Address: _____

Age: _____ Occupation: _____

Religion: _____

Attendance (Circle one) Regular   Occasional   Never

With whom are you living? List name, occupations and ages. If they are students, indicate grade level.

_____   _____
_____   _____
_____   _____
_____   _____

Marital Status (circle one) **single   engaged   married   remarried   divorced   widowed**

Developmental Information

How would you describe your home life growing up? Be specific and add a story or two to illustrate.

_____

_____

_____

_____

Health

How was your health in general in childhood? _____

_____

Any physical disabilities _____

Did you have any surgical operations? Please list them and at what age they occurred: _____

_____

Avocational Interests

Games and interests during childhood: (include make believe)

How is most of your free time occupied?

Explain:

Does any member of your family suffer from alcoholism, drug addiction, or anything that would be considered a "mental disorder"? **Explain:**

Please try to remember and list any fearful or distressing experiences.

Family Data

List all brothers and sisters, from oldest to youngest including yourself. Please list in birth order, including any miscarriages or abortions that you know of. List under each description listed below:

Name	**Sex**	**Age**	**Marital Status**	**Job**	**Describe Person**

Your relationship with your brothers and sisters?

Past:

Present:

Brother or sister most like you, in what respect?

Brother or sister most different from you, in what respect?

Did you experience any unusual achievements?

Self-Description

In what kinds of situations do you most readily lose self-control? (Cite particular instances if at all possible) Examples: lose temper, uncontrollable crying.

In which situations are you best able to maintain self-control? Give a word picture (description) of yourself as you would be described by your:

Spouse:

Your best friend:

Your worst enemy:

Your boss:

Your children:

Jesus:

Yourself:

List three strengths that you possess:

_____
_____
_____

List three weaknesses that you possess:

_____
_____
_____

What are you most important dreams/goals you have fulfilled/are yet to fulfill?

_____
_____
_____

Strategic Life and Coaching Plan
Key Areas to Explore

Physical (Health, Fitness, etc.)

Mental (Knowledge)

Social (Relational)

Spiritual

Strategic Life and Coaching Plan

Name:_____Date:_____

Area of Exploration:_____

_____

Goal:_____

_____

Objective 1:_____

_____

Objective 2: _____

_____

Objective 3: _____

_____

Frequency: _____

_____

_____   _____

Coach's Signature   Date

_____   _____

Printed Name   Date

_____   _____
Coach's Signature   Date

_____   _____
Printed Name   Date

About the Author

Dr. Stan DeKoven is the International President of Vision International University[10], and founder/President of the Vision International Training and Education Network.[11] Vision/VITEN specializes in establishing and supporting local, Church-based Bible Colleges and distance education programs. Through their unique "Bible College in a Box" system, they are presently serving more than 4,000 Resource Centers in over 150 countries and over 100,000 students through its affiliated ministries.

Stan has a diverse background in Education, Business, Military, Leadership and Counseling. He has pioneered two very successful businesses while consulting with others nationally and internationally. Stan has earned a Bachelors degree in Psychology from San Diego State University, a Masters degree in Counseling from Webster University, a Doctor of Ministry degree from Evangelical Theological Seminary and a Doctor of Philosophy in Counseling Psychology from the Professional School of Psychological Studies. Dr. DeKoven holds credentials in School Psychology, Marriage and Family Therapy, and clinical membership in many professional organizations. He specializes in Leadership development, and assisting executives achieve their potential in the marketplace. He is also an Executive Coaching Specialist for The

---

[10] Vision International University (www.vision.edu) is a California State Degree granting Institution, primarily offering their programs on line or direct distance (correspondence) and Church based programs. Vision has offered Associate-Doctorate, in Theology, Leadership, Counseling and Christian Education since 1989.

[11] The International Training and Education Network offers practical training in religious studies through the International Training College in over 140 nations, and in multiple languages, publishes Christian literature in multiple languages, and certifies ministers and counselors for service in an through the local church.

Vision Group, and the founder of Walk in Wisdom media ministries.

He is a licensed Marriage and Family Therapist in the State of California with over 35 years of professional services, specializing in:

- Crisis Ministry
- Domestic Violence and Recovery
- Substance Abuse Treatment
- General Family problems with children and Teens.
- Personal Coaching for men and women seeking improvement in vocation or relationship.

Credentials:

President: Vision International Education Services, Inc., sponsor of Vision International University
President: International Training and Education Network, sponsors of Vision Publishing, Walk in Wisdom Ministries and Family Care Services.
Former Associate Pastor: Christian Life Center; Senior Pastor, Vision Christian Church International
Clinical Director: Restoration Ranch
Member: Who's Who California and Outstanding Men of America
Certified Life and Executive Coach with the Institute for Motivational Living
Clinical Member: California and American Association of Marriage and Family Therapists
Clinical Member: American Christian Counselor Association
Chairman: International Association of Christian Counseling Professionals.
Certified Member of the American Chaplains Association

BOOKS BY DR. DEKOVEN:

Crisis Counseling

Family Violence: Patterns of Destruction

Substance Abuse Therapy

KingdomQuest: The Journey to Wholeness

New Beginnings: A Sure Foundation

Marriage and Family Life

On Belay! An Introduction to Christian Counseling

Group Dynamics

I Want to Be Like You, Dad: Breaking Free and Discovering the Father's Heart

Grief Relief

Parenting on Purpose

Old & New Testament Surveys

Fresh Manna (How to Study the Bible)

Leadership in the Church: In the Eye of the Storm

Visionary Leadership

Prelude to a Requiem: Principles of Leadership from the Upper Room

Supernatural Architecture (The Apostolic Church of 21st Century & Beyond)

And 20+ more books and booklets in various topics, see at www.booksbyvision.com

Dr Stan speaks on a wide range of topics from Christian Business, Christian Counseling, Leadership, Team Dynamics, Personal Coaching, Church Consultancy, Setting up Local Church Counseling, Teaching and Mission Ministries, World & Urban Missions, Youth, Church Structure and Personal and Corporate Vision.

Dr Stan assists many younger ministers develop in ministry and through speaking and consulting, giving relational oversight to churches both nationally and internationally. As such, He is in demand around the globe to speak in Leadership Conferences and to teach in Bible Colleges/Universities.

To schedule speaking or contact the author:

Vision International University: www.vision.edu
Walk in Wisdom Ministries: www.drstandekoven.com
drstandekoven@vision.edu
760-789-4700

www.ingramcontent.com/pod-product-compliance
Lightning Source LLC
Chambersburg PA
CBHW061313110426
42742CB00012BA/2163